Praise for
INSECURE AT LAST

"Highly personal, politically charged . . . a unique read that somehow manages to be both surprisingly uplifting and deeply unsettling."   —*Elle*

"Fresh, urgent . . . Ensler has put her money, passport and life's work where her mouth is."
—*The Washington Post*

"Brave, articulate, chilling, and inspiring."
—*O: The Oprah Magazine*

"Powerful . . . intimate and deeply moving . . . heart wrenching . . . Ensler is a master storyteller. . . . We close the book and can't stop thinking about it."
—*Arkansas Democrat-Gazette*

"Nobody brings sharp, witty, knowing voice to the plight of women in our country and the world like Ensler."
—*Marie Claire*

"Sensitive."   —*The Boston Globe*

"Moving . . . eloquent . . . highly recommended."
—*Library Journal*

INSECURE
AT LAST

ALSO BY EVE ENSLER

THE VAGINA MONOLOGUES

NECESSARY TARGETS

THE GOOD BODY

EDITED BY EVE ENSLER
AND MOLLIE DOYLE

A MEMORY, A MONOLOGUE,
A RANT, AND A PRAYER

INSECURE
AT LAST

LOSING IT
IN OUR SECURITY-
OBSESSED
WORLD

EVE ENSLER

VILLARD | NEW YORK

Published in the United States by Villard Books,
an imprint of The Random House Publishing Group,
a division of Random House, Inc., New York.

VILLARD and "V" CIRCLED Design are
registered trademarks of Random House, Inc.

Originally published in hardcover in the United States by
Villard Books, an imprint of The Random House Publishing Group,
a division of Random House, Inc., in 2006.

Grateful acknowledgment is made to HarperCollins Publishers, Inc.,
for permission to reprint the following two lines "Chase after money
and security / and your heart will never unclench" from *Tao Te Ching
by Lao Tzu: A New English Version* with Foreword and Notes by
Stephen Mitchell, translation copyright ©1988 by Stephen Mitchell.
Reprinted by permission of HarperCollins Publishers, Inc.

LIBRARY OF CONGRESS CATALOGING-IN-PUBLICATION DATA
Ensler, Eve.
Insecure at last: losing it in our security-obsessed world /
Eve Ensler.
p. cm.
ISBN 978-0-8129-7366-2
1. Women—History—21st century—Case studies.   2. Feminism—
Case studies.   3. Ensler, Eve.   I. Title.
HQ1155.E57 2006
305.4209'0511—dc22   2006046219

Printed in the United States of America

www.villard.com

2 4 6 8 9 7 5 3 1

Book design by Gretchen Achilles

FOR
MY SON, DYLAN

FOR
KIM AND PAULA

Chase after money and security
and your heart will never unclench.

—TAO TE CHING

(*translation by Stephen Mitchell*)

CONTENTS

III. LEAVING MY FATHER'S HOUSE

IV. FINALLY EXPOSED—INSECURE AT LAST

INTRODUCTION:
WORRIED ABOUT SECURITY

I am worried about this word, this notion—security. I see this word, hear this word, feel this word everywhere. Security check. Security watch. Security clearance. Why has all this focus on security made me feel so much more insecure? What does anyone mean when they speak of security? Why are we suddenly a nation and a people who strive for security above all else?

In fact, security is essentially elusive, impossible. We all die. We all get sick. We all get old. People leave us. People surprise us. People change us. Nothing is secure. And this is the good news. But only if you are not seeking security as the point of your life.

When security is paramount you can't travel very far or venture too far outside a certain circle. You can't allow too many conflicting ideas into your mind at one time, as they might confuse you or challenge you. You can't open yourself to new experiences, new people, and new ways of doing things. They might take you off course.

You can't not know who you are; it's more secure to cling to hard-matter identity. So you become a Christian or a Muslim or a Jew, you are an Indian, or an Egyptian or an Italian or an American. You are heterosexual or homosexual or you never have sex or at least that's what you say when you identify yourself. You become part of an US, and in order to be secure, you must defend against THEM. You cling to your land because it is your secure place, and you must fight anyone who encroaches on it.

You become your nation, you become your religion. You become whatever it is that will freeze you, numb you, and protect you from change or doubt. But all this does is shut down your mind. In reality, you are not a drop safer. A meteor could still fall from the sky, a tsunami could rise up next to your beach house, someone could fly a plane through your building.

All this striving for security has in fact made you much more insecure. Because now you have to watch out all the time. There are people not like you, people you now call enemies. You have places you cannot go, thoughts you cannot think, worlds you can no longer inhabit. So you spend your days fighting things off, defending your territory, and becoming more entrenched in your narrow thinking. Your days become devoted to protecting yourself. This becomes your mission. This is all you do. You collect canned goods or bottles of water. You find ways to get as much money as you can, and food and oil, in spite of how much you have to take from other people or the methods you have to devise in order to take it. You submit to security systems to check your pockets and IDs and bags. Every object becomes a potential weapon. One week it's tweezers, the next week it's rubber bands.

Of course you can no longer feel what another person feels because that might shatter your heart, contradict your stereotype, destroy the whole structure. Ideas get shorter—they become sound bites. There are evildoers and saviors. Criminals and victims. There are those who, if they are not with us, are against us.

It gets easier to hurt people because you do not feel what's inside them. It gets easier to lock them up, force them to be naked, humiliate them, occupy them, invade them, kill them—because they do not exist. They are merely obstacles to your security.

How did we, as Americans, come to be completely obsessed with our individual security and comfort above all else? What do we *think* we mean when we talk about security, and what do we *really* mean? Whose security are we talking about? Is it possible to live surrendering to the reality of insecurity, embracing it, allowing it to open us and transform us and be our teacher? What would we need in order to stop panick-

ing, clinging, consuming, and start opening, giving—
becoming more ourselves the less secure we realize we
actually are? How has the so-called war on terrorism
given rise to this mad national obsession for homeland
security, which has actually made us much more insecure at home and in the world?

In this book, I have gone back to chart the events
that have personally and politically led me to ask
these questions. I grew up in a middle-class family and
neighborhood in the United States. I had plenty of
food, clothes. I had my teeth straightened. I took ballet
classes. We went on vacations. I had a good education.

This security did not come for free. It was my father's money and he created reality. From early on, my
emotional and psychological well-being were sacrificed
for this economic security. My father was a raging alcoholic. His anger permeated and infected my world. His
fists, his hand, his belts, marked my young body and
my being. I was always ready to be hit or yelled at or
erased. I was told over and over how lucky I was to
have a nice house, to live in a good neighborhood. So
early on, I came to equate my economic security with
violence.

I never dreamed of growing up and getting married,
having children. Never. It simply didn't occur to me.
There were many reasons. One, I was born in the early
fifties and my consciousness was shaped in the sixties.
I was a hippie. I gravitated toward drugs, free love,

non-monogamy, communes, and anything that had to do with escaping the nuclear family. That nuclear unit was just that for me: nuclear—an atom bomb that annihilated my self, my worth, my confidence, and my identity. My father's rage, his power, his opinion, his money, his moods, controlled and determined all of us, including my mother. Our house, our family, was his empire. I was his subject. Or his tortured prisoner.

I never dreamed of growing up and getting married and having children because I never dreamed of growing up, living that long. I could never imagine life past thirty, and I came close to making sure I didn't get there. I never dreamed of having children, as I was so scared of repeating what had been done to me. I was so scared that I had my father in me. And in fact, I did. I held his rage, his impatience, and his judgments for many years.

It is not surprising that I have grown up to become nomadic. I was unable to have a dining room table until my early fifties, as it was the set piece of so much humiliation and violence. Until my late thirties I kept my bedroom out in the open in my living room so no one could get me. My dreams were limited, simple. All I wanted was to grow up and not be hit or molested. I lived as a survivor. Happy every day not to be screamed at, ridiculed, beaten, terrorized, or thrown out. I did not care about a career. I did not think what kind of a person might be right for me. It was all about what was *not* happening, all about the pain stopping, all about safety, security. I wanted a man or a woman who would not hit me. This, as you can well imagine, is not the greatest prerequisite for a relationship. Not a very high standard. And it's broad. And, to be honest, until you have gone back and retraced and experienced and purged and transformed that initial violation, it is impossible not to keep being attracted to what you are trying to escape.

I think you have several options when you experience enormous terror and violence as a child. You can shut down completely, you can pretend it didn't happen, you can become violent yourself, or you can create situations that mirror your initial situation in an attempt to understand and master it. I have, at some point, embraced all of these. My life has been a journey to find a way to make sense of violence and terror and make peace with insecurity.

In the last ten years I have traveled to many places—more than forty countries. Looking back, I see that a pattern emerges. I see how I was consistently and compulsively drawn to that which I feared, to those situations that seemed utterly incomprehensible. I see how this search to understand brutality and violence began as a search for logic and security but became the journey that freed me of the false need for these protections, dissolving my moorings, undoing my falsely constructed notions of security.

I have spent time in refugee camps, war-torn countries, battered-women and homeless shelters, prisons, border towns, and postdisaster sites. I have lived through a near plane crash, an almost bombing. I have left a fifteen-year relationship. I have embraced a weeping fifty-year-old man in his burnt-out backyard in Kosova. I have held the hand of a woman whose face was melted off by acid in Islamabad, Pakistan. I have clung to the body of an Afghan woman in the middle of a seizure as she remembered the torture and murder that took place in a stadium in Kabul. I have stood face-to-face with a raging member of the Taliban, his whip in hand as he prepared to flog me. I have watched the World Trade Center towers fall in my beloved city. I have sat with thousands of women from Srebrenica in a stadium as they wailed in grief over their lost men. I have spent days in dusty Ciudad Juárez, Mexico, searching for bodies of dead women, and in the hot sun of Crawford, Texas, as Cindy Sheehan stood up to President Bush.

I live alone today after cohabiting with partners for more than thirty years. Many of the vestiges that tied me to the ground, to one person, to one place, are gone. In fact, I have become a traveler, a woman who exists in motion, a nomadic being, a citizen of the world. I have been fortunate that the work I do has literally taken me around the planet. But travel is by no means a prerequisite to getting lost. We are able to cross and dissolve all kinds of borders if we are willing to go to the political, emotional, and spiritual places we most fear and resist.

I write and perform and I love my friends all over the world. I work to stop violence against women. I work to prevent and stop war. I sometimes have anxiety. I have bouts of terrible low self-esteem. I feel lonely on occasion, but mainly I feel alive, free. I feel myself.

This may or may not appeal to you—this moving, this nomadic existence, and this nonattached life. I am not suggesting we all leave our relationships and homes and children. Not at all. I am proposing that we reconceive the dream. That we consider what would happen if security were not the point of our existence. That we find freedom, aliveness, and power not from what contains, locates, or protects us but from what dissolves, reveals, and expands us.

I

DRAWN TO
WHAT I FEARED
THE MOST

THE FIRST MELTING

I t is difficult to determine where any journey really begins. From a very young age, I was suspicious of the promise of security. Walt Disney cartoons and *Father Knows Best* gave me enormous anxiety. I sensed an underworld that was not being expressed, and the absence of it made me nervous. As a teenager I read two books over and over: *Hiroshima* and *Death Be Not Proud*. In the first, John Hersey documents individual accounts of those who survived the first nuclear attack. I remember melting flesh, bookcases crushing an older Japanese man, radiation sickness, hair falling out. In the other book, John Gunther's son gradually and nobly dies of a brain tumor. I do not know which I feared more, nuclear annihilation or a massive tumor in my brain.

I remember when I became afraid of the dark. It was after I watched the movie *The Invisible Man* on television. There was something about Claude Rains unwrapping his bandages and revealing that underneath there was nothing, he was nothing. I vomited the whole night. I still feel nauseous thinking about it. The idea of becoming nothing, that we were made of nothing, the dissolution of self, of ego, was then my greatest fear. It was my introduction to death.

The possibility of tumors, disappearance, annihilation, circled my childhood, but it wasn't until I traveled to a war zone in my early thirties that the abstraction of insecurity became a reality. In spite of even my very difficult childhood, I still lived in a comfortable environment. I had a cozy house on a white middle-class street in the USA. There were no air raids. No curfews. There were no bombs dropping around me. There was no one dragging my mother or sister out to be murdered or raped.

Sometime in 1993 I was walking down a street in Manhattan when I was seized by a photograph on the cover of *Newsday*—six young Bosnian girls who had just been returned from a rape. A rape camp. A place where soldiers held kidnapped women to serve and pleasure them. A rape camp in 1993. It seemed utterly surreal and impossible. Yet the faces of the girls who had survived indicated the seriousness and reality of the situation. There was something about the anger in their faces, and the shock. There was something about the disassociation and the loss. These girls entered me. Or perhaps they already lived inside me. I knew I had to go and be with them. I didn't really know how or why. I knew I had to go and hear their stories. I had to know the details of what happened to them. I had to be close, to touch them, hear them, smell them, know them.

"They took my sixty-year-old mother and my sixty-eight-year-old father outside. These Chetniks, these boy soldiers who grew up with us, went to primary school with us. They were our neighbors, our close friends. They took my father first and made him stand in the center of our lawn. They were holding guns to his head. Then they casually began to throw stones, big stones, at him, pelting him in his head, his neck, his knees, his groin, as he stood helpless and very confused before us—before me, my mother, our other relatives. He was bruised and bleeding and exposed and they wouldn't stop."

I was sitting in a metal chair in a circle of women, all smoking and drinking thick black coffee from tiny cups, in a makeshift doctor's office in a refugee camp outside Zagreb, Croatia. I was listening to a thirty-year-old woman "doctress" (as my translator called her) describe her recent nightmare experiences in Bosnia. It was the summer of 1994. I had gone to Croatia for two months to interview Bosnian refugees.

"Then they took my mother and poured gasoline around her feet. For three hours they lit matches and held them as close to the gasoline as they possibly could. My mother turned pure white. It was very cold outside. There was nothing we could do. Three hours they tortured her like this. Then she started screaming. She was so courageous, my mother. She ripped her shirt open and screamed, 'Go ahead, you Chetniks. Kill me. Kill me. I am not afraid of you, not afraid to die. I am not afraid. Kill me. Kill me.' "

The group of refugees around me seemed to have stopped breathing or moving as they listened to this story. Except for their eyes, which filled up or fluttered reflexively from pain.

I heard myself asking reporter-like questions in a strange reporter-like voice, a voice that implied I had seen all this, it wasn't new, just another war story. I asked questions like "How do you explain your neighbors turning against you like that?" "Did you ever worry about being a Muslim before the war?" I asked these questions from behind this newly developed persona as if it were a secret shield, a point of logic, a place of safety. I was suddenly a "professional."

"After I had finally escaped and gotten here, I heard our village was safe again. The U.N. raided the concentration camp and my father was released. I began to get a glimmer of hope. Then the real horror happened. The Chetniks invaded my village. They were wild, insane. They butchered every member of my family with machetes. My mother and father were found, their limbs spread out all over our lawn."

I listened to the doctress's words and I felt the loss of gravity. Something caved in. Logic. Safety. Order. Ground. I didn't want to cry. Professionals didn't cry. Professionals asked questions and transcribed answers. Playwrights see people as characters. She is a doctor character. She is a strong resilient traumatized woman character. I choked back my tears. I bore down on the parts of my body where shakes were leaking out.

During my first ten days in Zagreb, I slept on a couch in the Center for Women War Victims. This was a remarkable place. Originally it had been created to serve Croatian, Muslim, Serbian women refugees who'd been raped in the war. Over three years it had evolved to serve more than five hundred refugee women who had been not only raped but shattered and made homeless by the war.

Most of the women who worked there were refugees themselves. They ran support groups, provided emergency aid: food, toiletries, medication, toys, et cetera. They helped women find employment, affordable medical treatment, schools for their children.

In those first ten days, I spent between five and eight hours a day interviewing women refugees in support groups in city centers, desolate refugee camps, and local cafés. I interviewed mothers, widows, grandmothers, lawyers, doctors, professors, farmers, teenagers. I heard stories of atrocities and cruelty. I met a country of women dressed in black: black silk blouses, black cotton skirts, black lycra T-shirts. The courage, community, kindness, and miraculous sense of forgiveness I witnessed on the part of these war victims threw me into moral chaos and deep questioning.

In all these interviews either I was filled with an overwhelming desire to rescue the women or I tried to maintain this "professional playwright" position. I was observing these women as characters, hearing their stories as potential plays, measuring the drama in terms of beats and momentum. This approach made me seem cold, impervious, superior. Both postures were attempts at maintaining a distance and, more important, maintaining my security.

Thousands of journalists had already passed through these women's lives. They had visited for a day, a week at most. The women felt invaded, robbed, ripped off. The reporters were interested only in the most sensationalistic aspects of these women's lives—the gang rapes, the rape camps. One journalist had actually sent a fax (these were still the days of faxes) saying, "Get me one raped woman, preferably gang raped, preferably English speaking." The women had taped the fax to the bulletin board as evidence and a warning.

It was a great honor and privilege that the refugee workers had brought me into the camps, allowed me to be in their most intimate groups. They had even, at times, focused their groups around my being there.

I felt I had not honored my end of the contract. I realized that if I wasn't "saving" these women—offering solutions—or transforming them into literary substance, I had no idea what to do. My ways of relating were hierarchical, one-sided, based on me perceiving myself as a healer, a problem solver. All of this was based on a desperate and hidden need to control—to protect myself from too much loss, chaos, pain, cruelty, and insanity. My need to analyze, interpret, even create art out of these war atrocities stemmed from my real inability to be *with* people, to be *with* their suffering, to listen, to feel, to be lost in the mess.

On the tenth day in Zagreb, a woman who worked at the center generously offered me her apartment for the weekend. I was actually terrified. It would be the first time I'd be alone since my arrival in Croatia, the first time I'd be able to digest the stories and atrocities.

In all my years as an activist—working in desolate shelters for homeless women, tying myself to fences to prevent nuclear war, sleeping in city parks in women's peace camps with rain and rats, camping on a windy Nevada nuclear-test site in radioactive dust—I had never felt so lonely. I called the States. I reached answering machines in place of loved ones. I paced the little apartment. I tried to read but was unable to concentrate. I lay down on the bed.

My heart was breaking from the inside like an organism giving birth to itself, to the stories of itself: the lit cigarettes almost put through the soldier's wife's eyeballs so "she could always see clearly," the decapitated heads of her old parents, the fifteen-year-old girl raped by her soldier husband and his soldier friends in the car, the hand grenades he stored in their house, the pistol they put in her three-month-old baby's little hand as a game, the food they didn't serve the Muslim girl's mother, who had decided to give birth to the baby of the Serb who raped her, the Canadian uncle who attempted to molest his fourteen-year-old niece who had fled to him from Sarajevo for safety, the dirty stained clothes that arrived in the bandaged boxes of humanitarian aid that the refugee women were supposed to be grateful for, the broken toys, the generic ammonia-smelling body soap, the husband and son she last saw two years ago digging the graves of friends and relatives in their village under orders from Serbs, the waiting, her twisted waiting face, the big fang-exposed German shepherd that the Chetniks held right near the little babies' faces in her living room as he forced the Muslim doctress to suck his dirty dick while her mother was forced to prepare his dinner, the window the twelve-year-old girl jumped out of eight stories high because she couldn't comprehend how her best friends from high school, her friends from the disco, had turned so quickly against them with knives, guns, fire, and insults, the cows they burned with bombs and left starving, the family cows.

Tears broke out of my eyes like glass cutting flesh, breaking me, breaking through my craving for definition, authority, fame, somebodyhood, breaking all that into little tiny pieces that became nothing I could identify, nothing that resembled me or the matter of me. Me was lost. There was just melting. Bandages unwrapping. Me becoming invisible.

It wasn't the cruelty that broke my heart. Cruelty is boring, generic. What hurt in my chest was witnessing the unsuspecting nature of the women, how unprepared they were, how shocked and disbelieving. What hurt was feeling love for these lost women who sat around a wobbly refugee table. The woman who clung to her one plastic bag or made sweet pastry in what was now her kitchen, bedroom, living room, bathroom, all in one. Made pastry for me, a stranger. The woman who kept smiling with missing teeth, who gave strength to the woman next to her, who smoked cigarettes and smoothed her skirt or apologized for her messy hair. What hurt was that their life was over. What hurt was that they kept going.

After this experience, my journey was transformed. I began to re-perceive the nature of my interviews, the nature of interviews in general. I began to see these encounters as sacred social contracts. I, the interviewer, could not simply take stories, events, feelings from my subjects. I could not sit there icy and objective, absorbing. I had to be present. I had to be in dialogue. I had to be insecure. I could no longer protect myself, stand outside the stories I was hearing. I had to allow myself to feel the sadness, torture, fear, loss, and particularly the courage and strength of the women I was meeting. War was not natural. I would never be comfortable with atrocity and cruelty. I found myself crying often during the interviews. I felt little, helpless. I experienced aspects of myself—defenses, identities, approaches—dying away.

I changed continents. I changed clothes. I went from a tiny village on the Adriatic where I visited Croatian refugees to the hot dusty Asian landscape of Pakistan, where I was covered in purple Indian cotton, the traditional salwar kameez. I was there to visit a group of Bosnian refugees who were living in dreadful circumstances. This particular group of Muslim men and women had previously lived in a hostel in Croatia. There they had been offered the choice of being moved either to a dangerous and overcrowded Muslim refugee camp close to the Serbian border or to Pakistan, where, they were promised, they could begin a new life of "bungalows, swimming pools, and jobs."

So about five hundred of them had come to Rawalpindi, Pakistan. The reality they found could hardly have been further from what had been promised. The temperature was 120 degrees Fahrenheit and higher during monsoon rainstorms. Initially they had to live thirteen people to a room. Malaria was rampant, as were diseases from the water and food.

The culture was radically different from their own. The majority of these Bosnians were Muslim, but they were more modern and Westernized than they were religious. Suddenly they were in a fundamentalist Islamic country.

Because their Pakistani hosts were offering them even more than they offered most of their own citizens, more than most countries had offered them anywhere in the world, the Bosnians felt guilty not feeling more grateful. They spent their days waiting—waiting for the weather to cool off, waiting to get out of Pakistan (those that were waiting for entry into America had been waiting the longest), waiting for news of their hometown, waiting for the nightmares to pass, waiting.

Each day I would sit with these refugees for many hours in a saunalike room; we would form a huge circle and the people would tell their stories. Everyone was sick in some way, everyone deeply traumatized from the horrific events they had suffered in the war. And yet, there was great humor, generosity, and community.

During my last days there, I became very ill with some kind of flu. The Bosnians overwhelmed me with kindness, offering me homemade remedies and soups. There was this particular little bottle of nose drops that had clearly passed through the entire community. When they offered it to me, I felt I was undergoing a rite of passage. Now I was infected with refugee illness, with a tiny bit of their suffering.

I had a fever and my nose was running. I felt all my defenses and protection had been washed away, and that didn't seem to matter anymore. I sat on a mattress in a 120-degree room while an older woman with shaking hands was telling her story.

"They came, a group of them, into our neighborhood. They took my first neighbor, my best friend, into the street. There were fifteen soldiers. There in front of her husband and children and neighbors they raped her one after the other until all fifteen had raped her. They did this in front of all of us. They did it to teach us a lesson.

"Please, tell people in America what happened here. We want them to know what happened here. We do not understand how they have abandoned us."

I asked her then, "Tell me, were they successful? Did the Serbs make the Muslims feel bad about being Muslim? Did they take their dignity and self-esteem?"

"No," she said. "No. Not. They raped many women. Twenty-two thousand women. They did not take our dignity though. They did not touch it. The women who were raped did not lose their dignity. What they lost was their minds."

I looked around and I realized a lot of us were crying, sweating, melting. In that moment I loved these Bosnians completely. I loved their stove-made bread and their meat-filled peppers that they cooked for us each day in the heat. I loved that they had survived and their hearts were intact and their kindness was so deeply present even now after everything. We got lost in each other's arms, we grieved their losses. We raged at the cruelty they had suffered. And in the center of this weeping, in the center of this sweating and running nose, I found an odd, perfect strength. It is the strength that comes from surrender, from dissolving.

I returned to the States on a plane that nearly crashed over the Atlantic. In midflight it simply dropped thousands of feet out of the sky. Passengers went flying, luggage was released from the overhead compartments, and objects were hurling through space. Parents were rocking their children. Many were praying and chanting, some were crying, others were perfectly still. The woman next to me took my hand and said she needed to tell someone goodbye. We were walking through our final moment. Then somehow the falling stopped, the plane got caught on some ledge of air.

Flight attendants had brain concussions. Passengers had spiritual experiences they felt compelled to share with strangers.

————

Eventually I came back to earth—well, the plane landed. In fact, something crucial inside me had changed. Sure footing was gone. I had seen how easily neighbors and supposed friends could turn against their friends and neighbors. I had seen how in a split second a comfortable life could become a nightmare. I had seen how quickly fascist thugs could rise to power by manipulating the people with tactics of racism and terror.

Suddenly nothing was secure. Nothing was dependable. Nothing was what it appeared to be. My life in the U.S. seemed bizarre and irrelevant for months afterward. Most of me remained in Croatia and Pakistan with those women. The memory of their stories and faces and beings made my falsely constructed and misdirected life impossible. I was completely disoriented, unwilling and unable to participate in business as usual. The deconstruction of the notion of security threw me into the center of sadness, rage, and a torrent of other emotions. Oddly though, I was not depressed. Lost, searching, emotional, but not depressed. It had been my denial itself, not the painful things I had been denying, that had been depressing and isolating me. It had been my clinging to what I instinctively knew were lies and illusions that had reduced and imprisoned me.

WHEN I LEARNED THAT BULLETS
ARE FROZEN TEARS

My trip to the former Yugoslavia had opened the world for me, and my hunger for the world. In doing so, it undid the contained, safe borders of my existence. Suddenly a woman weeping over her lost son in an image on the front page of *The New York Times* was no longer a theoretical entity. She was real, a woman I might have met, might have known. I was connected to her. I could no longer divorce myself from her pain, her suffering.

Initially this was overwhelming. I had nightmares. I felt restless and wrong in my comfortable life in America. Everything seemed absurd and pointless. I came to understand why we block out the pain and atrocities of others. That pain, if we allow it to enter us, makes our lives impossible. It forces us to examine our own values and reality. It insists that we be responsible for others. It thrusts us into the messy world where there are no easy solutions or reasons, only struggles and questions. It creates great fissures in the landscape of our insulated, so-called safe reality. Fissures that, once split open, can never close again. It compels us to act.

When I began traveling I was utterly terrified of flying. Not only did I have consuming claustrophobia, I had no understanding of how a plane could possibly stay in the air. I had seen every air-disaster movie. My flight home from Pakistan only made the fear worse. Flying was all about giving up control, turning my security over to someone else, to the pilot, to the winds, to overworked traffic controllers, to hijackers, to turbulence, to chance (suicide bombers came later).

Flying became my practice where I faced my fear of death, where I learned to die into the turbulence and hours suspended in space. My need to travel, my need to know, my need to be free, slowly became stronger than my fear of crashing.

In the next years I went back quite a few times to Croatia and then Bosnia. I became involved with several women's peace groups there. I made lasting friendships with women throughout the Balkans. It was logical that I ended up in Kosova.

There were many things about my trip to Kosova in 1999 that would have made anyone uneasy. Returning with my two friends to their apartment in Priština right after the war ended, not knowing what we would find. The mouse poop everywhere, the missing electronic items, the sense that enemy soldiers had been sleeping in their bed and peeing on their rugs. The general wreck of what was once their home. Or the roads that we drove on for days, still laced with land mines. The potential for explosion and death heightening every moment, making it surreal, making us hysterical.

Or meeting Marta in a café. The humility and heroics of this petite woman, the simple telling of her story.

"There was a village, Little Krushe. On the second day of the NATO bombing, the Serbs forced everyone out of their houses in this village. They separated men from women. There were a hundred sixteen men. They took the men, put them in four lines, and shot them. The women and children could hear the machine guns. Then they told the women, 'You have three choices: go drown yourself in the river, go to Albania, or we shoot you here.' My village was on the other side of the Drini River. I just happened to be looking out my window with binoculars. I saw smoke rising over Krushe. The village was burning. I saw hundreds of women and children at the bank of the river, screaming, waving frantically for help."

Marta got her younger brother, Toma, and their big tractor and went to the river. Marta's mother was shouting after her, "Why do you have to be the first one?" It was very dangerous. There was shelling all around. Women were screaming and crying. "I cannot describe how much," Marta told me. "It was difficult to calm them down. I said, 'Don't lose your hope.' Everyone wanted to get on the tractor. Some crying, 'How can we get on? We don't know where our sons and our fathers are.' I said, 'Be patient. Don't be afraid. We will get every one of you across the river. I promise.' The river was high. We made fifteen trips. Most of the villagers in my village came down. They brought another tractor and took women into our village.

"I was never afraid. It was very important to save the lives of the children. More important than my own life. In those moments you become strong—there is an old saying, 'A human is stronger than stone.' " There was an old woman, very heavy. Marta and her brother had to crawl back to get her. They brought her across the river. She told them her brother, husband, son-in-law, nephew, and brother-in-law had all been killed in the massacre.

They took women and children into the clinic in their village. Two women had been wounded by shells. One of the women had given birth two days before. High blood pressure. All of them traumatized. All the writing on the medicines was in a foreign language. Marta managed. "The people from villages all around came to me and said, What are we going to do? No Kosova Liberation Army, no government. They came to

me for answers. I'm just a teacher, headmistress, activist.

"We kept women in our village. Four days later, the
Serbs arrived and said we were hiding refugees. They
threatened to kill us. So we said we were all leaving.
We all left with the women and went to Albania. Later,
some of these women's families came from Germany
and other places to the camps in Albania to thank me
personally.

"There was a young girl, Violeta. Her father had
been with the men who were shot. She was so sad she
wanted to stay in her village. I tried to stay very close to
her. I kept saying, 'Maybe he was one of the survivors.'
We had heard four men had survived and hidden in the
mountains. A few days later they appeared. When Violeta saw her father covered in mud and blood and realized he was alive, she hugged me. She couldn't bear to
hug her father."

Our uneasiness in Kosova could have come from returning to the Drini River with Marta, returning to the
scene of the event. A strangely beautiful muddy river.
Boys were swimming in it. The day grew hotter. When
we arrived, a group of about thirty boys and men came
to greet us. A NATO helicopter flew overhead as they
did in Kosova what felt like every fifteen minutes. The
boys waved enthusiastically. The villagers showed us
the part of the river where the event took place. They

said the river was higher that day. They posed for a photograph. The boys wrestled to be closest to Marta.

They told us there was a problem. Bodies were washing up on the riverbanks, and no one was coming to check them. They had been told to leave bodies until they were identified, but dogs were taking parts of the bodies and bringing them into the village. Could we help them identify, photograph the bodies?

We walked through the fields, a group of us, by the river. Trying not to reveal my panic, I asked casually if the fields were mined. The villagers pointed to the cattle. "The cows graze here," they said with utter detachment. "They seem to be fine. No one has blown up yet."

Suddenly the villagers stopped. A skull, a leg bone, a jawbone, shoes, clothes alongside a scummy pond. There might be more bodies in the water. The uneasiness could have come from standing there right next to a human skull. A skull that just a few weeks or months ago had been a man, a human being. He was looking at this river, maybe, or eating or thinking about the heat.

Being this close to bone and death or the possibility of being blown apart would have certainly been enough to break me, pierce through my illusions of security, but it was something else, something surprising, that got me.

After leaving the river we went to a nearby village called Magura to see if we could help with supplies. Houses on the road were charred and mangled.

We found Sylvie, who was forty-eight, in her back-yard. She had lost everything during the war, including her sight. Sylvie's vision had always been bad, but the morning after long-haired Serb paramilitaries had broken into her house and held guns to her head, she woke up and discovered she was blind. Then she fled to Albania with the rest of the women. When she returned, the girls in the village debated whether they should tell her what her house looked like, about the extent of the damage. She had lived there her whole life; her father and grandfather had lived there before her.

The paramilitaries had shat and pissed on her family's clothes. They had written Serbian graffiti on the freezer. In all her photographs, they had cut off the heads of her family. They had taken everything—carpets, sofas, pictures. They had sprayed the house with gasoline. They had set it on fire. It had exploded. Now there were knee-deep piles of rubble in every room. A broken teapot, a little red purse, a box spring. Charred reminders.

Sylvie, her eight-year-old son, and her old mother were all living on the ground outside. They didn't even have anything to sleep on. Neither of Sylvie's two brothers, who were close to her age, had been heard from since the war. When Sylvie's mother talked about them, her whole body shook. "If only, if only I could see my sons before I die. If only they would come home."

We all walked together through the broken house. Then we sat on the ground outside. We promised we would come back with mattresses and blankets.

None of us slept that night. We were haunted by the thought of a frail grandmother being forced to sleep on the ground in the backyard of what was once her house.

We went back the next day with supplies. As we arrived, we heard a huge commotion in the yard. The grandmother was crying out and Sylvie was clinging to a man. When they saw us, the commotion got louder. They cried out to us, "It is a miracle, he just walked in, he just came home, he has found us."

Her son Agim was a big man, strong, muscular, dark-haired, in his forties. He seemed paralyzed—unable to move or talk. Maybe it was our arriving at that moment and being witnesses, maybe it was his hearing I was from the United States, but for some reason he looked at me, threw his arms around my neck, and started weeping. No, it was more like wailing. I have never heard a sound like that. He would not let go. The wailing grew louder. I sat down in order to hold him better, and he buried himself in my arms. Then this weeping wailing began to build and release. It could not be controlled or stopped. It resounded through the neighborhood. People from the village began to gather around.

I held on to Agim, but inside, honestly, I wanted him to stop. All these years I had told myself I wanted men to be vulnerable, to have their feelings, to cry. All of a sudden it felt like a lie. I did not want this man to be so destroyed, so out of control. I wanted him to have answers and be tough and know the way and make everything work out. I understood how part of me was afraid of men being lost, how I needed them to be tough and sure. I understood how many years I had carried their invisible pain so I wouldn't have to see them weak or ashamed. This weeping liquid man in my arms was my undoing, pulling me out to sea in the wild waves of his crying

The wailing went on. His body shook and thrashed about. It was as if I were holding the secret story of men in my lap. Centuries of male sorrow and loss, centuries of unexpressed worry and doubt, centuries of pain. I suddenly understood violence and war. I understood retaliation and revenge. I understood how deep the agony is and how its suppression has made men into other things. I understood that these tears falling down Agim's face would have become bullets in any other case, hardened drops of grief and rage directed toward a needed enemy. I saw how, in fighting to live up to the tyranny of masculinity, men become driven to do anything to prove they are neither tender, nor weak, nor insecure. They are forced to cage and kill the feminine within their own beings and consequently in the world.

Which is what brought me to Afghanistan.

ALMOST FLOGGED

t was 1999 and I had heard how the women in Afghanistan were not able to leave their houses, how they weren't allowed to go to school or have jobs, how they weren't allowed to sing or dance, how they were beaten for wearing the wrong-colored socks. I had heard how they were forced to be covered any time they were in public and that some were sick from lack of exposure to the sun. There was something about the lack of outrage surrounding the state of Afghan women, something about the acceptance of it, that made me fear for the future of all women.

Freshta was twenty-six, thin, pale, and haunted. She was an undercover reporter who traveled across Afghanistan and risked her life to document the atrocities of the Taliban, the fundamentalist Muslim regime that controlled her home country.

"On Fridays," Freshta said, "the Taliban closes the shops and streets in Kabul and forces all the people, children included, into a stadium. There they must watch as thieves have their hands cut off and are hanged from trees. Yet the Taliban is what has made these people so poor they must steal. I have seen women stoned to death in the stadium for refusing arranged marriages."

She reported on other atrocities. A six-year-old girl was beaten for carrying schoolbooks in public. Two cousins, a boy and a girl, were buried alive for talking in the bazaar. Commanders abducted and raped girls. "The girls don't want to be interviewed," Freshta said, "because they are ashamed. I interview their mothers, who usually say, 'Our daughters are dead to us.' "

Freshta told me that since she became a reporter, she had started fainting all the time. But that didn't stop her. "As long as I have the ability to publicize the shocking situation of my people, I will continue. I hope I will live to see the elimination of these criminals."

Freshta reported for the newsletter and website of RAWA, the Revolutionary Association of the Women of Afghanistan. More than two thousand members of this clandestine network provided shelter, education, and medical services to Afghan women and girls—all in defiance of the Taliban. Unable to show their faces in their own country, they built international connections through their website. I found them by e-mail.

After interviewing me at a hotel in Peshawar, Pakistan, and making sure I was trustworthy, RAWA's leaders agreed to show me their schools and orphanages. They helped secure me passage into Afghanistan to witness firsthand life under the Taliban.

My journey began in Pakistan, home to 1.2 million refugees who had fled the Taliban.

In a city I agreed not to name, a driver sympathetic to RAWA's mission took us down narrow, garbage-strewn streets until we reached an unmarked house. Behind a gate, unseen from the street, a guard armed with a machine gun stood watch. He let us inside, where we found clean, ordered classrooms decorated with brightly colored pillows.

RAWA operated a dozen schools like this one in Pakistan, some in desert refugee camps and others in RAWA members' own houses. In Afghanistan itself, RAWA ran sixty-five schools and thirty-three orphanages, all housed secretly in private homes. In Pakistan, the schools faced harassment and raids by Taliban sympathizers. But in Afghanistan, both students and teachers risked death. RAWA rotated school locations and strictly limited class sizes to avoid detection.

The women studying at the school I visited, refugees of every age, told me their stories in turn. "A member of the Taliban struck me with a stick because I wasn't wearing a burqa," said a manic forty-eight-year-old widow, referring to the long Afghan garment that provides only a small opening for air and sight. "I fell facedown on a stone. No operation will fix it." She showed me her knee, swollen and deformed. Various women showed me scars of whips on their bodies, mainly their ankles.

Then the women brought out a television and VCR and put in a videotape. They were nervous and edgy. Freshta had smuggled the camera under her veil into a stadium in Kabul. On the screen we saw about nine Taliban men arrive at the stadium in the back of a Toyota pickup truck. Soon, another truck appeared carrying three women covered in burqas. A man with a microphone read from the Koran.

One of the women was led into the center of the stadium and thrown to the ground. A Taliban man placed his gun to her head and, without pause, fired it. We never even saw her face. Wails and cries filled the stadium, but the dead woman was left on the ground like garbage. As the video went on, the wailing continued. It took me several moments to realize that it was coming from the room I was in. Then Freshta suddenly lurched into my arms in convulsions. Watching the video had restimulated the trauma she had witnessed in the stadium, and she no longer had her camera between her and the horror. Her body was flailing and thrashing about. As I tried to hold her and comfort her, the retraumatization spread instantly through the room. Women were crying and agitated. Suddenly

Freshta's four-year-old daughter, having heard her mother's cries, came running into the room. The underlying world of stress, sorrow, and terror that women lived with became apparent.

RAWA's founder, a poet and activist named Meena Keshwar Kamal, was twenty years old when she formed the group in 1977 in hopes of gaining equal rights for Afghan women. At the time, this cause was not yet life-or-death. Women were earning Ph.D.'s and working as doctors, lawyers, and teachers. If they wore the burqa, it was out of religious preference, not in enforced obedience to national law.

But in 1979 Soviet troops invaded the country to back the communist government then in power, and Islamic and tribal groups known as jihadi mounted armed opposition. When RAWA staged public protests opposing the communists and the jihadi with equal passion, Meena paid for it with her life. In 1987 she was killed in her home in Quetta, Pakistan, by the Afghan KGB and their fundamentalist accomplices. After her death, RAWA members went underground, determined to complete what their leader had begun.

After Meena's assassination, RAWA had no single leader—that would leave them too vulnerable. Instead, the group has been directed by a rotating council of twelve women. Men support, protect, love, and marry RAWA members, but they cannot join the organization. Watched over by bodyguards, the council meets every three months, both in and outside of Afghanistan. At the end of each meeting, members decide where they will next convene. They tell no one else of their plans.

In Pakistan, we met journalists who had been waiting many months to get into Afghanistan. But we were very lucky. Within a week, after an extraordinary intervention on our behalf by the International Rescue Committee, we secured the visas we needed. We were escorted by Sunita, a sweet twenty-year-old woman who had been on only one other mission for RAWA in Afghanistan. If questioned, we agreed to say that we were tourists and Sunita was our translator. Sunita was required to don the suffocating burqa. As a foreigner, I was permitted to cover myself with a scarf instead. Notebooks, cameras, and cell phones were banned, but we brought the first two anyway. An armed Pakistani policeman traveled with us through the Khyber Pass to protect us from bandits on the road. When checkpoint officials along the route through the Himalayas seemed ready to turn us away, he waved his Russian-made machine gun and they let us through.

At the border, however, Taliban guards forced us out of our car. They claimed we did not have the right permit for the car, so we had to leave it. So we actually walked across the border into Afghanistan, our luggage in tow. At the Afghani border, there were Taliban members doing interviews and checking IDs. I got picked to do the talking. A large, intimidating man asked me why

I had come to Afghanistan. I mumbled something about the country being in my dreams, that I had always felt an affinity for it. He asked me what I was doing there. I stumbled and said I was a playwright and I was interested in theater. He stared at me and said, "There is no theater in Afghanistan. There is only the Koran." I said something really stupid like "Well, that will be interesting as well." I was sure I had totally blown it, but for some reason, he let us pass.

We hired a new driver, who loaded us into a decrepit station wagon and took us a long way through the desert to Jalalabad. Fortunately I was fairly ignorant about Afghanistan then and learned only later that this city was the stronghold of al-Qaeda. There we checked in to a hotel. Like all public lodgings, it was run by the Taliban—and, judging from the urinal in our bathroom, we were probably the first women to ever stay there. On the entrance to the hotel there was a sign with an image of a machine gun and a huge X through it. Leave your AK-47's at the door.

Sunita set up a covert RAWA meeting for that evening so we could meet the women who were doing the underground work. We covered ourselves in burqas in an attempt to blend in and avoid being followed. Three of us, under miles of fabric, squeezed into a tiny cab, smaller than a golf cart. Almost immediately the heat became unbearable, and I gasped for breath. I tried to be brave, but it was useless. I am insanely claustrophobic.

We took a circuitous route to a RAWA school, a house indistinguishable from the impoverished dwellings that surrounded it. A young teacher told me that thirty-five small classes were held there, teaching science, math, and reading. The literacy rate among women in Afghanistan was now 4 percent, she told me. Without education, there was no hope of raising a generation strong enough to defy the Taliban.

"The students arrive at different times, one by one," explained the teacher. "If someone knocks on the door, we hide the blackboard. The students have so much interest in school. Most don't know it's run by RAWA—but they know that if the Taliban sees them learning, they could die."

I interviewed the women. They were teachers. They were devoted. They knew the price for teaching was flogging or death by execution. They risked their lives so the future of the women in their country might be secure.

Then, abruptly, the interviews ended. We were told in hushed tones that we had to go immediately. That if we were seen outside after the 9 P.M. curfew, there would be trouble. The women hugged and kissed us again and again. They pleaded with us to tell their stories to the world, but they had no self-pity.

I had heard that the Taliban beat women who ate ice cream in public. Sometimes they even beat them if they ate it under their burqa. It was perceived to be lascivious and lewd. This haunted me. I couldn't stop bringing it up. Finally Sunita told me they were going to give me a special treat and take me to the secret ice-cream-eating place for women.

We walked through a crowded bazaar and into a broken-down restaurant. In the back, sheets were hung from the ceiling to create a makeshift room. Sunita and I walked in and sat down, and the sheets were pulled around us.

We waited nervously as the terrified restaurant owners watched outside and then, when the moment was right, arrived with bowls of vanilla ice cream. I watched Sunita lift her burqa and slowly and carefully eat the cool, sweet ice cream. In that moment she became a child—in the time before women were locked away without schools or jobs, when they could still laugh and see the sky. For that moment, no one had control over her. Sunita and the women of Afghanistan had, in the midst of total oppression and brutality, found a way to keep their pleasure and desire alive. She savored a few mouthfuls. Then we were warned that Taliban men were circling the bazaar in their Toyota pickups. We pulled down our burqas and the sweet taste and daylight were gone.

Some part of me feared I would never get out of Afghanistan. And indeed, as we drove back to Pakistan a few days later, our car was stopped by a member of the dreaded Department for the Promotion of Virtue and Prevention of Vice (DPVPV). He was huge, a mass of long hair and a dirty beard. I had stopped wearing the burqa in the car, and he caught me with a small scarf on my head. He ordered me out of the car. He was clutching a wooden paddle, attached to which was a long, flat, wide leather whip used for flogging. I recalled the black-and-blue ankles of the woman I met at that first RAWA school, and the way she still had trouble walking. He was raging and screaming in a language I didn't speak but totally understood. I went into a kind of disassociated place that was calmly and oddly familiar. I thought of women living like this every day and having no recourse or way out. I felt the insane powerlessness, the rage at his mean, indifferent ugliness. I realized that I could die there or be severely beaten.

It was in this moment that I came to understand misogyny in my body and being. I understood how quickly and easily women could be treated as animals. I understood that the situation of those women was unacceptable and that, if allowed to continue, it would impact all of us, because that kind of brutality left unchecked creates an environment of inhumanity that is contagious. The pleas and protestations from our driver somehow saved me, and the mad flogger waved us on with disgust.

When I returned to the United States, I brought Freshta's videotape and an article I had written about my experience in Afghanistan to several TV stations and major publications. With the exception of one magazine, *Marie Claire,* I could not engender any interest in the story. No one could understand what the terrible plight of Afghan women had to do with their own interests, their own comfort and security.

UNDER THE BURQA

This poem is for the brave, tender, fierce women of Afghanistan, who not only survived but kept their country alive. Wearing a burqa should obviously be a matter of culture and choice. This piece is about a time and place when women had no choice.

Imagine a huge dark piece of cloth
hung over your entire body
like you are a shameful statue.
Imagine there's only a drop of light,
enough to know there is still daylight for others.
Imagine it's hot, very hot.
Imagine you are encased in cloth,
drowning in fabric, in darkness.
Imagine you are begging in this bedspread,
reaching out your hand
which must remained covered, unpolished, unseen
or they might smash it or cut it off.

Imagine no one is putting rubles
in your invisible hand
because no one can see your face
so you do not exist.

Imagine you cannot find your children
because they came for your husband—
the only man you ever loved
even though
it was an arranged marriage
because they came and shot him
and you tried to defend him and they trampled you,
four men on your back
in front of your screaming children.

Imagine you go mad
but you do not know you are mad
because you are living under a bedspread
and you haven't seen the sun in years
and you've lost your way
and you remember your two daughters vaguely
like a dream the way you remember sky.

Imagine muttering as a way of talking
because words do not form anymore in the darkness.

Imagine you do not cry because it gets too hot and
*   wet in there.*

Imagine bearded men that you can only decipher
by their smell
beating you because your socks

are white.
Imagine being flogged
beaten in the streets
in front of people you cannot see.
Imagine being humiliated so deeply
that there is no face attached to it
and no air. It gets darker there.
Imagine no peripheral vision
so like a wounded animal
you cannot defend yourself
or even duck from the sideward blows.
Imagine that laughter is banned
throughout your country, and music,
and the only sounds you hear
are the muffled sounds of the muezzin
or the cries of other women flogged
inside their cloth, inside their dark.
Imagine you can no longer distinguish
between living and dying
so you stop trying to kill yourself
because it would be redundant.
Imagine you have no place to live
your only roof is the cloth
as you wander the streets
and this tomb
is getting smaller and smellier every day
and you are beginning to walk into things.
Imagine suffocating while you are still breathing.

Imagine muttering and screaming
inside a cage
and no one is hearing.
Imagine me inside the inside
of the darkness in you.
I am caught there
I am lost there
inside the cloth
that is your head
inside the dark we share.

Imagine you can see me.
I was beautiful once.
Big dark eyes.

You would know me.

THEY BLEW HER UP 'CAUSE THEY
COULD NOT CUT HER DOWN

was surprised when I saw my stomach in the barely standing full-length mirror in my room at the Intercontinental Hotel in Kabul, surprised that my stomach was not huge. It was lean, but lean the way an older body looks lean. It was not clean-lean. I was surprised that it was not full—pouring out. Full of the dust that had fallen and continued to fall over everything, full of the cold, shivering impoverishment that crept deep into one's skin, full of the loss—there was nothing green, nothing whole, nothing working, nothing dependable here. Full of the stupidity that had leveled concrete, shattered glass, smashed wood. There were very few roofs. There was nothing to eat.

Full of the stories. Stories like thoughtless episodes that come out of nowhere and undo everything forever. The story the orphan girl told of the Taliban breaking into her family's house in Mazar-e Sharif.

They had been eating dinner. The Taliban insisted, as they often did, that her father build a fire to make them warm and her mother go quickly and cook for them. Her brother was sent to get petrol for the gas stove. The mother anxiously set about cooking. Nothing was moving fast enough. Her brother rushed with the gas and accidentally dropped it on the floor, which started a fire. The Taliban, now convinced the family was mocking them, trying to set them on fire, argued outside with the father, who was desperate to convince them it was an accident and return to his screaming son, now on fire in the living room. The son was completely burned. The father rushed into the house too late and burned most of his upper body trying to save what was left of his son. He was unable to work ever again. The mother lost her mind.

Or the story of the bomb that fell accidentally from an open car door into the river. Several weeks later, an orphan girl's brother, who was her twin and her best friend, came upon the bomb while playing in the water with his friends. They wrestled with it and rode it and brought it out of the river. It exploded in their hands, blowing them each to pieces.

Stories. Full of stories, full of the emptiness that comes when hope, the reason for tomorrow, is blown away. Full of the smells that remain after everything is charred. Full of the body, the female body, that goes on anyway, despite madness, despite losing one's husband, despite dust. Full of misery.

I looked at my stomach in the full-length mirror that could shatter as everything else had. My stomach, which usually had instincts or at the very least hunches, was now mute, not knowing anything, stunned by the massive acts of cruelty. Twenty-three years of cruelty. Stunned into utter submission.

I was starving and there was nothing to eat. There was nothing that would make this better. Unless we were to start over again as a species, were able to admit that we had spun off in the wrong direction. Were able to just stop. But I wondered if even that would make things better, would remove the mark of cruelty, the stain of violence, in the cellular structure—this stain that now directed and redirected everything. We are products of violence, each and every one of us. We are its outcome and its creation.

Here in Kabul, the dust had gathered. It got so deeply and quickly into your lungs that it had created something called the Kabul cough. What was left after the buildings and mosques and people were gone got into your lungs, making you cough and gag. Here in this history of invasion, usurpation, domination, obliteration, interrogation, the dust was the new weather. When it rained, the dust became mud. When there was heat, a thermal lining.

We walked through a public garden, thick in mud.
The soldiers who stood outside to guard it guided us
through. It was as if they were now guarding a memory, a knowledge of another time in Kabul that was luscious and green, when the almond groves and apple
trees and roses were alive in the sun, and the dancing
rooms and the theater thrived. The soldiers guarding
this story walked us around, pointed out what was
once there. You could smell the greenness, and even
though most of the trees were skeletons and stumped,
you could remember their blooming. The soldiers became tender, proud, when they described the dancing,
when they told of the days of joy. But those days were
not days they remembered. They had been born into
dust. It was the memory of their parents, or their parents' parents, that they needed to trust. These soldiers,
no more than twenty-one, had never lived without the
Kabul cough. It was like an allergy. You got used to it.

They walked us around until we came upon what
had once been the most beautiful tree in the garden. We stood around its charred remains. An open,
wounded, blackened trunk in the ground. It had once
been the grandest tree of all. When the Taliban took the
garden, they had chopped down most of the ancient
trees for kindling to keep themselves warm. They had
tried to chop this tree, but it would not come down.
So, one night, they put a bomb in the trunk and blew it
up. Blew it up—the most beautiful, the grandest and

greenest, the most luscious, the holder-of-hope tree. They blew her up. Now there was a blackened-out hole in the ground.

I remembered this tree. Or maybe it was my mother's memory or her mother's memory. Someone must remember before there were land mines and guns and bombs. Someone must remember before the dust seemed so familiar, before this dust seemed like the future.

The soldiers blew her up 'cause they could not cut her down.

I held fast to the memory of greenness as I coughed. I saw the garden alive. I held fast to my belief that we will one day survive the beauty. That we will surrender to it rather than blow it up.

DUST

I was not shocked by September 11. I was saddened and disturbed by an attack on my beloved city and people, but not shocked, not surprised. It was the dust. I knew that dust that seemed to consume the space that was once the World Trade Center towers, that began to waft its way through the island, seeping into my bedroom in Chelsea at night, filling me with the taste and smell and feel of the dead. I had tasted that dust before, found it covering my shoes, lining my backpack, coating my clothes and mouth in Kabul, in Bosnia, in Kosova. This dust is not new to many people of the world. They live in it, build their homes out of it, die from diseases that come from it. They make space for it, become inured to it.

The economic policies and military actions of the U.S. have been responsible for spreading this dust in Chile, Nicaragua, Somalia, Grenada, Afghanistan, Iraq, El Salvador. America has supported regimes and despots and fundamentalists who have produced tons of this dust in their own countries with American dollars and weapons. But this dust had never before dirtied our streets, never filled our lungs. September 11 changed all that. The remains of the Twin Towers blew through Manhattan and became our first taste of global sorrow, misery, and violence on our own soil.

I remember lying in my bed, this sorrow lining the roof of my mouth. I remember waiting for another attack, sitting straight up in the middle of the night, anticipating chemical gas and immediate suffocation. But I also remember, in the midst of the terror, feeling an odd sense of recognition. The illusion of security was gone. Now we in America could join the rest of the world in a kind of existential, political reckoning. Years of American policy of aggression and invasion and occupation had come back at us. The insane disproportion of wealth and resources in the U.S. had come back on us. The disregard and indifference to the suffering of the poor and sick in the world had come back on us. I was enveloped by grief and fear, but I felt a door opening. Finally we as Americans would see our role in creating animosity and hatred, we would be forced to examine our history and our hegemonic policies and imperialism and our indifference. This would be a time of accountability, a time of transformation and truth telling.

For days after the attack, my apartment became

open space for hundreds of friends and activists who craved community, who needed to talk and cry and worry and strategize together. Not one person who came to my house, not one person I met on the streets of New York, had any interest in revenge. Something had opened in us. Suddenly we were tender and vulnerable and real. In all our discussion there was deep examination of history, a drawing out of the why of the attacks, a deep concern about brutal fundamentalism, a curiosity about underlying causes.

People seemed far less afraid of a second attack than they were of the Bush administration. We hoped, naïvely, that there would be examination rather than revenge, reflection rather than retaliation. We stood, New Yorkers at Ground Zero, hungry not for more killing but for understanding. We wanted to transform this terrible poison into medicine, to allow the pain and loss to unite us with millions of others all over the globe who had been through the same or much worse. We formed a group, New Yorkers Say No to War. We held vigils in Union Square Park, which was transformed into a site for ongoing mourning and resistance to war. Thousands joined in. Hundreds of thousands marched through the city. We grieved.

The U.S. government went in exactly the opposite direction. Government reports and announcements evoked fear and terror on an hourly basis. American pain was pronounced as the single most important pain in the world. We were the special ones, the privileged. Attacks did not happen in our country. Our security was the only thing that mattered. Or this is what the government told us in order to justify its rise to power and control. And Americans went along, because the terror was used as a tool to beat them into compliance. Once the Bush regime had paralyzed enough of the country in terror, anything could be done in the name of security. They could call these particular attacks "war" even though they were the work of a few state-less criminals. They could decide to drop bombs on Afghanistan even though they had no idea where al-Qaeda forces actually were in Afghanistan. They could say that the murder of poor Afghan women and children was collateral damage, necessary for American security. They could use the liberation of Afghan women as a pretext for bombings even though they had never been interested in the liberation of American women, nor had they been interested in the situation of women in Afghanistan months before (nor would they be after). They could manufacture false connections between these terrorists and Iraq to justify a major war, a war they had been planning to launch long before September 11. They could openly lie, and Congress, which should have been vigilant and fierce in finding the truth, would be passive and bullied by words like "patriotism" and "traitor." In the name of security, they could build detention centers and hold prisoners illegally. They could curtail civil liberties. They could justify no longer abiding by the Geneva Conventions. They could invent an "Axis of Evil" and define evildoers and saints. They could justify and order torture.

Like a chip, the myth of security got implanted into the American psyche. Every time the government got questioned or criticized, every time they wanted to move their agenda forward, the chip got sparked and the population got shocked and then behaved as told because they were so afraid of another attack.

The irony, of course, is that security was never part of this administration's real agenda. This is revealed in the outcome. In 2004, in the time of supposed security under the Bush regime, more terrorist attacks occurred in the world than at any time since 1985, more nations elected governments openly opposed to the U.S., more terrorist youth were born out of humiliation, rage, and shame, more faith and hope were lost in the promise of U.S.–style democracy worldwide. The Department of Homeland Security has revealed itself to be utterly unprepared, inept, and unresponsive. If we look at the response to Hurricane Katrina, a catastrophe that came with advance warning, we see that they were not only insanely unprepared but shamefully unwilling to organize an effective response.

Security has been used by this administration as a cover
for the consolidation of its power and control. If we
cling to this addictive illusion of security, we keep ourselves blind, and by doing so, we abandon responsibility for the future, leaving it in the hands of the reckless
and tyrannical.

On September 12, 2001, I was thinking about violence. About an airplane full of terrified women and
men and children smashing into a tower full of unsuspecting women and men who were just sipping their
morning coffee. The burning people jumping from the
one hundreth floor, jumping for their lives. The hundreds of firefighters and police officers who were lost,
crushed under a collapsing tower. The husband waiting
in his office for fourteen hours for his wife who worked
on the 104th floor, his wife who had not called, who
was probably never going to call, and yet he was still
waiting. The man who called his mother from the hi-
jacked plane to tell her he loved her, to tell her to remember he loved her. The debris and the dust on New
Yorkers' shoes and how protected we had been. The
people who were driven to hijack airplanes with knives
and box cutters and fly them through buildings, who
were ready, eager, to lose their lives to hurt other people. Why? What would make people want to do that? I
was thinking about people all over the world who secretly applaud those hijackers because they live in

squalor and poverty and desperation and rage at the governments and corporations and banks who have stolen their world out from under them. I was thinking about the words "retaliation" and "punishment," "security" and "act of war." About the hardening that comes from any form of fundamentalism. About violence, what it feels like to be nothing to someone else. What it feels like to be a consequence of someone else's dissociated rage, disconnected fury. About the cycle of hurt for hurt, nation against nation, tit for tat.

I was thinking about falling. Falling. How falling can become grieving, not knowing can become sorrow. How not knowing can become change. How helplessness can be the beginning. How falling is not shooting. Not bombing. Not knowing. Not stopping. How falling was what some chose that day. Instead of burning.

GOING THE DISTANCE

With millions of others on the planet, I marched against the looming war on Iraq. I marched in London, I marched in New York, I marched in Rome and Delhi. We marched because for that moment we all knew the insane devastation and future that would follow such a war. We all knew a lie was motivating the war, we all knew the absurd injustice of launching a war on a country that had not attacked or even threatened to attack us. We suspected the war would make the world even more unstable and that thousands of Iraqi women and children and men would die and thousands of U.S. soldiers would lose their minds and lives.

Sometimes I think about what we *didn't* do, the millions of us. Marching is a comfortable, secure way to protest, isn't it? You go out for the day in the streets and walk and make noise and feel righteous and indignant. You feel the solidarity with the others who are righteous and indignant. You listen to some speeches. You pound some drums. Chant some antiwar rhetoric. Then you go home and have dinner or take a nap or watch the march on TV or get drunk.

But we all knew what would follow if we didn't stop the war. We knew the bombing would destroy the infrastructure of Iraq and ruin the water and the electricity. We knew the invasion would create more rage and bitterness. And that the rage and bitterness would eventually become human bombs. We knew that once the U.S. got started, they would justify staying in Iraq and killing more and more Iraqis, more and more U.S. soldiers. We knew civil war would eventually follow. We knew women would be raped and robbed of their rights. We knew the war was always about oil and profit for the corporations at the great expense of the Iraqi people. We knew there was no plan for rebuilding after all the destruction.

We knew all of this. *So why weren't we willing to lose everything to stop it?* Why didn't we move into the streets? Why didn't we wail at the gates? Why didn't we put our bodies on the line? Why didn't we stop everything we were doing? Why didn't we go the distance?

Security.

———

Cindy Sheehan went the distance. She left home. She put her body on the ground, on Crawford, Texas, soil. She wailed at President Bush's gates. She stopped her life to stop the war. She gave up everything that was known and secure. And yes, they came after her. They slandered her and lied and attacked her character. And of course she was hurt and lonely and afraid.

But because she went all the way, she made a space for others to follow. She made it possible. When I met her in Crawford, she was literally camped out in a gutter on the side of a hot dusty road. She was there with a few hundred others. You could say it was crazy there, dangerous, totally insecure. Or you could say they were pushing the boundaries out far enough so the rest could begin to get free.

"The first dream I had after I found out Casey was dead was on the morning of Mother's Day. There's a big stage. It's clearly a special event. Casey's walking toward me. I am so happy to see him. He's carrying a 7-Up in one hand and a rifle in the other. He's walking nonchalantly, like he always did. He puts the rifle in his mouth and shoots himself. I fall to the ground screaming, 'Why did the Army make Casey kill himself? Why did they do it?' "

We were sitting in Cindy Sheehan's donated trailer

in Crawford at the end of a long, hot, complicated August day. The local sheriff had asked Cindy to move here from her tent at the campsite down the road, now called Camp Casey, so he would sleep better not worrying about her safety. The trailer was full of women supporters. There were peace activists, mothers who had lost their children, volunteers, and Cindy's younger sister, Dede Miller. One of the women cooked a late dinner of rice and beans. Another gave a detailed account of the size and variety of her bug bites. Another outlined a press response to the day's assault on Cindy's character. Dede nursed a sunburned face. She was bragging about how Cindy, forty-eight, had always been a leader, always been bossy. But never like this. She pointed to Cindy: "I do not recognize that masked woman!"

Cindy was doing about four things at once, but nothing was strained or rushed. She talked to me about her dreams with her computer perched on her lap— once she wrote her nightly blog, she got up to go to sleep. She drank a beer. She laughed at Jon Stewart on *The Daily Show* doing a spoof: Cindy, Camp Casey, and George Bush. She agreed with her sister that she was bossy. "But I was never bossy with my children," she said. "I never yelled. I never told them what to do."

Three weeks earlier Cindy Sheehan had come to Crawford from her home in Vacaville, California, to meet with President Bush while he was on his vacation. She wanted one hour to talk with him about the death of her son Casey, twenty-four, in Iraq. She wanted to know why the president continued to call Casey's death noble and "why he lied to the American people about the existence of weapons of mass destruction in Iraq." More than anything, Cindy wanted accountability.

The next morning, at around nine, I found Cindy in her pajamas, sitting outside her trailer on a lawn chair, wrapped in a comforter. She had been up for hours talking to an early-morning TV show.

I asked her to tell me about Casey and how he died. "Well," she said, "I guess we're going to start the morning off with a good cry.

"I never wanted Casey to enlist. No one in our family supported the president or believed in this war. The Army recruiters found Casey at Vacaville High School. They went for him relentlessly. They made so many promises. Eventually they got him. They told him he would get a twenty-thousand-dollar signing bonus. He got forty-five hundred. They promised a laptop. It never came. They promised he would finish college while in the service. He never took a class. They promised he would be a chaplain's assistant. The position was filled when he got to boot camp. Instead he was assigned to be a Humvee mechanic. Casey did not believe in the war. He wanted the future that the Army promised, and he was loyal. He was an honor student, an altar boy, and an Eagle Scout. Once he made a commitment, he honored it, and he stood by his buddies."

Cindy had had terrible anxiety during the first five days that Casey was in Iraq. Until April 4, 2004. That was the first morning she woke up without a sense of doom and dread. It was like something had been released in her. It felt odd and it panicked her. She had a day off from her job as an administrator at the Napa County Department of Health and Human Services. She went to brunch with her friend and drank mimosas to try to calm this uncomfortable feeling.

"That evening I was watching the five o'clock news with my husband, Patrick," she told me. "We were eating filet mignon and grilled vegetables. The news said that eight soldiers were killed in Baghdad, and they showed a Humvee burning. I said one of those boys is Casey. My husband said, 'He just got to Iraq. You're gonna need to get some help, if you're gonna worry like this.' I said, I know Casey is dead. Then I tried to block it out, convince myself he was only wounded. I went out to walk the dogs.

"I came home and there were three Army officers in my kitchen. I knew right away. The officers waited for me to return before they told the news. I remember my husband had just done this huge batch of laundry and he was standing there holding a pair of pants. He told me later that the first thing he thought was, 'My poor wife.' Everything was frozen. I dropped to my knees and started screaming and screaming, 'Why Casey? Why my Casey?' It was the closest I have ever come to dying without dying. It was so violent."

Carly, her twenty-four-year-old daughter, was at home. Andy, who was twenty-one, was at his house. Jane, nineteen, was at work. "We called them and told them to come home. I made the Army officers leave the house before they got there. My husband told my daughter Jane, and she started hitting him, saying, 'Shut up. Shut up. You're a liar. You're a liar.' I went into the kitchen. My three kids had their arms around each other and they were sobbing.

"Casey was my oldest. We all loved his laugh. My kids never knew life without their big brother.

"My husband and I had been together thirty-one years. We went in different directions after Casey's death. His way of grieving was to distract himself. He told me to get a hobby instead of immersing myself. But there was nothing else I could think about. He told me I was sick. He was a big part of bringing Casey into the world, but he didn't carry him inside or nourish him. He didn't nurse him. I touched every part of Casey and he touched every part of me. He was attached to my body.

"With a broken heart, there is true physical pain. I cried myself to sleep. I cried in my sleep. I would wake up with a sore throat from crying. My husband didn't always want it in his face so much. He and other friends

were constantly telling me to get on with my life. Many
nights, I was in so much pain, I would have to fight to
keep from taking the whole bottle of sleeping pills. I
might have gone down that road if my daughter hadn't
written this poem:

A NATION ROCKED TO SLEEP

*Have you ever heard the sound of a mother screaming for
    her son?*
*The torrential rains of a mother's weeping will never
    be done.*
They call him a hero, you should be glad that he's one,
*but have you ever heard the sound of a mother screaming
    for her son?*

"I asked myself how I could sit there wallowing
when I could work to keep other women from having
to go through this pain. I didn't make the world better
for Casey." She started to cry. "Now I'm going to try."

Shortly after Casey was killed, Cindy joined Military
Families Speak Out, an organization for families with
children in Iraq. She began to travel and speak about
her feelings against the war. But it was a meeting with
President George W. Bush that propelled her into outrage and radical action.

"In June 2004, nine weeks after we buried Casey, I
was still in deep shock and pain. We were invited to

meet with the president in Fort Lewis, Washington. We were alone in the room with him. He was rude and cold to us. 'Mr. President,' I said, 'what are we doing here? Why did you invite us to come here? We are lifelong Democrats.' He said, 'Mom, it's not about politics.' He said he felt our pain. He clearly didn't even know my name. He went up to my daughter Carly and asked who the loved one was to her. She said, 'Casey was my brother.' He said, 'I wish we could bring your loved one back.' She said, 'So do we.' He said, 'I'm sure you do.'

"It took me months to process that meeting. I realized later that he met with us privately 'cause he was hiding the war. He has never attended one single funeral of a fallen soldier.

"My son is a war victim, not a hero. What is noble about what he's done? Going in and invading a country that is not a threat to the U.S.? That is not noble. What would a noble cause be? What would I want my children to die for? I believe there is always a peaceful solution. If people are wise enough, careful enough. Saving a baby from a burning building is noble."

Six months later, in January 2005, Cindy, who had never been an activist before, founded Gold Star Families for Peace, a group for families who had lost their loved ones in war. It was both a support group and an antiwar group.

"Contrary to what the mainstream media thinks, I did not just fall off a pumpkin truck in Crawford, Texas, on that scorchingly hot day three weeks ago. I have been writing, speaking, testifying in front of congressional committees, lobbying Congress, and doing interviews for over a year now."

On Wednesday, August 3, Cindy decided to go to Crawford. Two days later she announced it spontaneously when she was speaking at a Veterans for Peace conference in Dallas. She asked if there was anyone at the conference who would drive her there. It was that unpremeditated.

"I didn't think that far ahead," Cindy said. "I thought it would be me and my friend Diane. I knew my sister could stay for a day. I planned to be here for a month. This"—she gestured in the direction of Camp Casey—"is what you call unintended consequences. The country was ready for it." A *Newsweek* poll taken in August 2005 revealed that 64 percent of Americans did not believe the war had made them safer. Sixty-one percent said they disapproved of how the president was handling the war. "The kindling was there," Cindy said. "This was way bigger than me." I asked her what in her own personal history she called upon to take on the president. She said simply, "Being a mother."

More than five thousand people have passed through the site. The night I was there I attended a candlelight vigil with a few hundred people in front of a wide pink twilight sky. All over the planet, at seventeen hundred vigils, one hundred thousand people joined us.

Thousands of letters and e-mails poured in daily. Most of them celebrated Cindy. Some were just addressed to The Woman in a Crawford Ditch. People sent money from their Social Security checks. They sent peanut butter and toilets and long-stemmed red roses. Cindy and the camp have received more mainstream-media attention in America than the fifteen million people who marched around the world trying to prevent the Iraq war. Sure it was August and things were slow, so the media were willing to pay attention. But there was something about the simplicity of Cindy Sheehan. The right-wing media accused her of scheming and strategizing, but as one camper said, if they think someone organized this, they should just live at Camp Casey for a few days.

At Camp Casey, in a pasture outside Waco, there were hundreds of white wooden crosses in the ground, each with the name of a slain soldier. Hundreds of Cindy's supporters—veterans from the Iraq and Vietnam wars, local folks from all over Texas, priests and ministers and rabbis, students and families for peace, a group of farmers, mothers who have lost their children in Iraq—had traveled far to stand with her. One woman whose son died in Al-Falluja said to me, "The worst thing for a mother is to lose a child. Hardest thing not to jump in the grave with them. Our sons and daughters were so honorable. Used by people who would not go to war themselves. They played G.I. Joe with my kid's life. Cindy speaks for us. We are all Cindy."

If something negative happened at Camp Casey, so did its miraculous opposite. In mid-August, a man mowed down the crosses with a pickup truck, but within hours they were repainted and restored by the community at the camp and local police. One man fired his gun in the air to scare off protesters, but two days later his third cousin offered Cindy his private land for the whole camp.

I asked Cindy how her children felt about what she was doing here. She said, "They all openly support and believe in me. Jane and Carly are in Europe for the summer. They called the other night to say I was all over Europe and they were so proud of me." Cindy won't let Andy come to Texas, since the media are already overwhelming him in California.

I asked her how she's been able to handle the vicious attacks waged daily in the press and on radio and TV. She laughed and said, "You know—sticks and stones . . . water off a duck's back." Then she paused and said, "Sometimes I have to cry." She paused again. "But, really, I go to the positive things that are happening. I do not beat myself up. Strength is going out there every day when people are actively trying to discredit me. When they hate me. Being able to get out of bed when Casey isn't in the world. Rush Limbaugh said I'm not real. He said Casey's not real, that my story's based on forged documents. Does he think I buried an empty coffin?"

I asked her if the rumors are true that her divorce papers were served to her at her tent. She said her divorce had been in process for a long time and Patrick made a point of telling the lawyer not to serve them during this time. The lawyer didn't listen. The papers were filed in Napa County. She wasn't served in Texas. I asked her if she made anti-Semitic remarks about Israel's involvement in the war, as the press had accused. She said, "I didn't say it. I didn't think it. It isn't true." I asked how she felt when the columnists and TV pundits said she was being used by the "left." She said, "It makes me feel insulted that they don't think I can speak for myself. I have been speaking out for months. Are they saying that just because I am a grieving mother I can't have my own idea?" I started to ask about her in-laws, who didn't approve of her activities, but I caught myself. It felt like a rhetorical question. Who doesn't have trouble with their in-laws?

They could try to delegitimize Cindy by making her seem extreme or saying that she cusses or that she was being controlled or that she was treasonous. But really, there was something disarmingly unneurotic about her. I watched her walk through the camp, tanned, strong, exposed, and vulnerable, hugging young men who had just returned from Baghdad, telling jokes to the now familiar sheriff, or weeping with another mourning mother. You can't erase her by turning her into a hero, a madwoman, or an icon. Her sincerity, experience, commitment, and sorrow refused this. She remained profoundly and disturbingly one of us. "Cindy is a mother lion protecting her young," her sister Dede said. "She lost one and she is not going to let it happen to anyone else."

A few nights later, Cindy told me, a soldier came to Camp Casey and said that he thought Cindy should accept Casey's death and the war, that it was wrong to complain, that she should get over it. Cindy took him aside, away from the reporters. They spoke quietly for a bit, head-to-head. The soldier then confessed to Cindy that if he had died, his mother would be there doing the same exact thing as Cindy. Then, in front of the press, he hugged her. He looked her in the eyes and called her "Mom."

There was a deeply relaxed quality about Cindy in the midst of this storm. It was as if she had traveled to another place both internally and externally. She had a determination and a clarity. She could not be moved.

"You rely on institutions to tell you what to do," Cindy said. "I let the government take my son. You rely on institutions for rules and regulations, but all you have is yourself. Casey's death forced me to break out of all the known institutions: it ended my marriage, dealt the final blow to my belief in the Church (this had been coming for a long time), propelled me to stand up to take on the government, and completely changed my relationship to motherhood. Everything for me now is out of love, not duty.

"Since Casey's death moved me to action, I know I am on the right path. I hardly ever get sick. I have energy. Just need a few hours of sleep. I have never been more alive. My son brought me here. We all knew Casey was going to be a great man; we just thought he would be alive when it happened. I had no idea what a great man he would be. All this is happening now because of Casey. Casey and I gave birth to each other. His death forced me, freed me, to be the best human I can be, to be a true mother. If hundreds of women got free like this, there would be no war. How long are we going to keep letting the men kill our children? I hope it will stop right now."

In January 2006 Cindy Sheehan was arrested at President Bush's State of the Union speech for wearing a T-shirt that read, 2245, HOW MANY MORE HAVE TO DIE? (2,245 indicated the number of U.S. soliders who had already died in Iraq.)

She had been invited to the event by a congresswoman so that a mother who had lost a son in Iraq, who did not support Bush's prowar policies, could be present. As she unzipped her jacket in her seat, a policeman screamed, "Protester!"

He grabbed her and dragged her out of the hall. He used excessive force, bending back her arms, creating muscle spasms that continued to hurt her for weeks afterward. He screamed publicly for people to get "out of the way, out of the way," humiliating her by making it seem she was a dangerous person. She was held in prison for four hours. She is currently suing the U.S. government for violating her civil rights.

When your goal is security, anyone who disagrees with you becomes a threat. A grieving mother, wearing a T-shirt, whose son has sacrificed his life for war, gets treated like a criminal.

II

UNRAVELING

VAGINAS—MORE TERRIFYING
THAN SCUD MISSILES

think somewhere deep inside, a part of me always longed to get lost, to be taken, to be undone. I think my insane intake of drugs and alcohol and my wild promiscuity when I was younger were the manifestation of this longing. Sex is the way we practice dissolution, the way we rehearse our undoing, our surrender. It is how we free ourselves from the binding of duality, open to the endless world of ambiguity and pleasure. It is not surprising that sexuality is so repressed in America. It is not surprising that it feels more dangerous than bombs.

I had been a playwright for more than twenty years. I'd written plays about nuclear war, homeless women, incest, death, S&M, and Bosnia. I'd written about these particular issues because they were the things I most feared. I had learned early on that whatever secretly terrifies me ultimately controls me—determines how I feel, think, and behave. Confronting these terrors head-on had often lifted me from paralyzing depression and a sense of malignant helplessness. I felt oddly protected by my guerrilla-girl nature, my willingness to go to the scariest places, my activist way of working.

Nothing prepared me for vaginas. Vaginas were different. They snuck up on me, took me sideways, slowly consumed me, cell by cell.

It was an accidental possession. I started talking to a few women friends about their vaginas in 1994. By 1998, I'd interviewed more than two hundred women and performed their stories all over the world, from Oklahoma to Jerusalem, Texas to London. I'd performed in Zagreb at the antifascist theater and in Jerusalem, where there is no Hebrew word for "vagina." I'd performed at colleges, recital halls, Off-Broadway, in back rooms and private homes.

I did not realize the full potential and viability of the theater when I began *The Vagina Monologues*. I had certainly experienced the magic and the power before, but I had yet to understand its truly sacred nature, its ability to explode trauma, create public discourse, empower people on the deepest political and spiritual levels, and ultimately move them to action.

I believe in the power and mystery of naming things. Language has the capacity to transform our cells, rearrange our learned patterns of behavior, and redirect

our thinking. I believe in naming what's right in front
of us because that is often what is most invisible. By
saying "vagina" often enough and loud enough in
places where it was not supposed to be said, we made
the saying of it both political and mystical and gave
birth to a worldwide movement to end violence against
women called V-Day. In the course of nine years this
grassroots movement has spread, woman to woman, to
eighty-one countries. It has raised more than thirty-five
million dollars. It has helped open safe houses in Africa,
Egypt, Iraq, Afghanistan, and the U.S. It has moved
thousands into the streets, changed laws, saved lives. It
has released the word "vagina" in more than forty-five
languages. The public utterance of a banished word,
which represented a buried, neglected, dishonored part
of the body, was a door opening, an energy exploding,
a story unraveling. And yes, it began with the word, saying the word, because the word holds the memory, the
suffering, the shame, and the possibility.

It all began in a conversation with a woman friend
when she stumbled onto the subject of sex and meno-
pause. Out of nowhere, she began to talk about her
vagina. "It's dead," she said. "Dried up, ugly, finished."
She went on in detail. It was the bitterness of her tone,
her self-hatred and contempt, that spun me into an al-
tered state, a state I often enter when my politically
correct fantasy version of reality is deconstructed in

front of me, when I am propelled out of my denial and falsely constructed security and forced to see reality in all its brutal nakedness.

The woman who was speaking was deep and insightful. A self-proclaimed feminist, she was a great artist, a smart businesswoman, at the top of her form. And there she was hating her vagina.

I clung to my denial. I decided she was not like other women. She was aberrant. There had been a women's movement, after all. We had all been down there with our hand mirrors and speculums. We had come to love our bodies.

Yet, in spite of my denial, a door had cracked open, some wicked thought had broken loose. I had to explore further. I began to talk to women. Each conversation challenged my prescribed notion of who I thought women were and what they should be feeling. Each interview opened questions and dilemmas, knocked down more of the walls that protected my denial.

When I first began to perform these monologues around the world, I realized that just saying the word "vagina" caused enormous controversy, because "vagina" is, in fact, the most isolated, reviled word in any language. You can find words like "nuclear," "scud," or "plutonium" on the front pages of newspapers and they never cause anywhere near such a stir.

The taboo on the word is no accident. As long as we

cannot say "vagina," vaginas do not exist. They remain isolated and unprotected. Young girls get genitally mutilated and sex-trafficked throughout the world. Women get raped, burned with acid, and beaten, and no one is held accountable.

This is where theater comes in. Theater insists that we inhabit the present tense—not the virtual tense or the politically correct tense. Theater demands that we truly be where we are. By being there together, we are able to confront the seemingly impossible, we are able to feel that which we fear might destroy us—and we are educated and transformed by that act.

Theater is sacred because it allows us, it encourages us, as a community of strangers, to go someplace together and face the issues and realities we simply cannot face alone. Alone, we are powerless, translating our suffering and struggle into our own private narcissistic injuries. When we become a group, these issues become social or political concerns, responsibilities, a reason for being here together.

When I performed *The Vagina Monologues* in Oklahoma, a young woman fainted and fell to the floor after the Bosnia rape piece. We stopped the show, turned on the lights, got cold water. It turned out that the woman had been raped by her stepfather and she was overcome with memories. In the context of that theater, her suffering became our suffering. Audience members held her and spoke gently to her. Her abuse was contextualized and legitimized, as her personal history suddenly became part of a larger social order that oppressed all women.

There is this notion that if we really let ourselves think about all the terrible things in the world, we'll be depressed and paralyzed. It's true: thinking from a detached, sound-bite position is crippling. We become undone by the overwhelming masses of horrifying, objective facts and information.

But theater is not objective. It is there to invite us into the human experience more deeply—to inhabit others, to experience ambiguity, compassion. Each night that I performed *The Vagina Monologues*, I inhabited the monologue of the seventy-two-year-old woman who stopped having sex in her twenties when a date humiliated her. I entered the monologue of a wild lawyer-turned-dominatrix. I lived in the despair of the young girl who survived a rape camp in Bosnia. I experienced their joy and pain. But the pain did not paralyze me. Instead, it included me, expanded me, made me more than myself.

My experience has led me to believe that only by wholly entering, wholly feeling, wholly inhabiting other people and experiences, are we brought to any happiness and security. Only by allowing ourselves to see what we already see and know what we already know are we freed from depression and ennui.

This is possible in the theater if we are willing to strip away the layers, risk making ourselves uncomfortable, insecure for a time, risk saying the word "vagina" if that's the word that needs to be said.

THE DOOR THAT BLEW OPEN

So much of my experience with *The Vagina Monologues* was out of my control. So much of it felt as mystical and inexplicable as vaginas themselves. So much of it was about being taken and unraveled.

It was as if I had been standing in front of an ancient door, a door I had unconsciously longed to open and enter. Inside was a world I somehow knew but was scared to really know. When I uttered this sacred, taboo word—"vagina"—when I said it over and over—"vagina, vagina, vagina"—when I uttered it in public, sent it out into the collective sphere, the door finally blew open.

There were stories behind this door. I wanted them to be stories of healthy, satisfied love and sex and comfort and pleasure and intimacy. I wanted them to be stories about deep multiple orgasms and clitoral knowledge. Stories where women's bodies had been cherished and pleasured and fulfilled. There were some of these stories. But most of the stories were of pain, violation, and dissociation. The door that blew open was the door to the dark story, the buried story, the untold story of violence, of betrayal. Wherever I went with the show, women would line up afterward to tell me their stories. Stories of date rape and incest and humiliation. Stories of women who had never seen their vagina or never had orgasms or only faked them. Stories of women who were afraid of their vaginas, who hated their smell, who felt too wet or too dry. Stories of women who longed for it to be slow or not so rough and hard but were too afraid to ask. Stories of women who only wanted it hard and rough. Stories of women who could only have sex with strangers and stories of women who hated sex. Stories of women who got too anxious when someone actually focused on them.

I knew there was violence toward women, but I had no idea there was a worldwide epidemic. I had no idea of the centrality of the issue. I had no idea that one out of every three women will be beaten or raped in her lifetime. I had no idea how violence against women determined women's ability to think and remember and hold facts and organize information. I had no idea how it made them afraid to be touched, how it robbed them of agency over their own body, how it made their body someone else's damaged property—dirty, unsafe. How it tainted pleasure and perverted mystery. I had no idea how it made women shy and mute. How it made them strangers to people they loved, made them permanently homeless, emotional refugees. How it led to fatal diseases like AIDS directly contracted from perpetrators, or heart disease and cancer that emerged years later from the lasting impact of trauma. I had no idea how it made women afraid and bitter and hateful toward their sons, and jealous and overly protective and angry at their daughters. I had no idea how it brought women to prisons and homeless shelters. I had no idea how lonely it made women, how full of shame and self-hatred. How it spurred alcoholism and drug addiction and overeating and starving and compulsive sex. I had no idea.

When I traveled with *The Vagina Monologues* this ancient door blew open. I did not think I wanted this door open. I did not think I wanted to know such suffering. But if I told myself the truth, I already knew this suffering. It lived inside me, making me despairing and alienated and alone. We all know and hold the pain around us whether we realize it or not. It becomes disease or bitterness or cruelty or numbness if we are not conscious of it.

I remember in the Reagan years when the streets of New York City were filled with homeless people. Every day I would walk past lonely, scared, hungry people. Most of the time, I acted as if they weren't there. I learned to not see them, not hear their need. This act of

denying people required enormous energy. It required
me to be less of a person every day. Then a friend, a
photographer, asked me to come work at a homeless
shelter for women. She had been going to support
them and help them out. I did not want to go. I did not
want to know these women or their pain. I did not want
to feel guilty or engulfed by their circumstances. I did
not want to see how careless this whole system is for
so many, how easy it is to fall through the cracks. I did
not want to recognize the truth of that insecurity. I
resisted for months. As I resisted, I became more depressed, less present, less alive. It was only after going
to that shelter on Thirtieth Street, allowing these
women, their struggles and stories, into my being, that
I woke up. Suddenly I was not living in a separate reality, compartmentalized and falsely secure.

The stories, the violence, the desire, utterly destabi-
lized my life. But ironically, it was this unraveling that
compelled me to devote myself to ending violence
again women. And this commitment was indeed what
gave me life.

Over these ten years I have been privileged to travel
to the center of the story of violence against women. I
have been in crumbling shelters in the backstreets of
Cairo, in makeshift centers for teenage girls and women
in Jerusalem, Johannesburg, Pine Ridge, and Watts, in
mansions in Hollywood, in burnt-out backyards in Kosova and Kabul, in a moving van after midnight with

sex-trafficked girls in Paris. Sometimes these meetings went on for hours; sometimes, as in the case of the seventeen-year-old Bulgarian sex slave, it was just thirty-five minutes before her pimp came looking for her. I have heard the staggering stories of violence—war rapes, gang rapes, date rapes, licensed rapes, family rapes.

I have seen firsthand the scars of brutality—black eyes, cigarette holes in arms and legs, a melted face, bruises, slices, and broken bones. I have witnessed women living without sky, sun, a roof, food, parents, a clitoris, freedom. I have been there when skulls washed up on riverbanks and naked mutilated female bodies were discovered in ditches. I have seen the worst. The worst lives in my body.

But in each and every case I was escorted, transformed, and transported by one specific guide—a visionary, an activist, an outrageous fighter and dreamer. I have come to know these women (and sometimes men) as Vagina Warriors.

It was Zoya who first took me to the muddy Afghan camps in Pakistan; Rada who translated the stories of women refugees as we traveled through war-torn Bosnia; Megan who led pro-vagina cheers on a freezing cold campus in Michigan; Igo who made jokes about land mines as we sped in her jeep through the postwar roads outside Priština, Kosova; Rania, the stunningly beautiful and famous talk-show host from Saudi Arabia, beaten by her competitive husband, who showed her face publicly and changed the culture; CC who spoke out heart-stopping poems about her pain and triumph in a blues club on the South Side of Chicago; Calpernia and Andrea who brought transsexual women together publicly to organize against the secret violence perpetrated on their bodies and beings; Monique and Rossana who honored the Comfort Women in a stadium of 3,500 in the Philippines; the Comfort Women themselves, dressed in white, between seventy and ninety years old, who risked exile and shame to break fifty years of silence by telling of the rapes and atrocities done to them by Japanese soldiers.

At first I thought this was just a rare group of individuals, women who had been violated themselves or had witnessed so much suffering they had no choice but to act. But six years and almost forty countries later, I see a pattern that reveals an evolving species.

There is a growing population of men and women all over the world who are no longer beholden to social customs or inhibited by taboos. They are not afraid to be alone, not afraid to be ridiculed or attacked. The illusion of security was shattered at some point in each of their lives, so they are no longer bound or controlled by the promise of it. They are willing to face anything for the safety and freedom of others. Call them grassroots activists, call them revolutionaries. Call them Vagina Warriors.

They are everywhere. In a time of escalating and explosive violence on the planet, these warriors are fostering a new paradigm.

Although Vagina Warriors are highly original, they possess some general defining characteristics:

They are fierce, obsessed, and can't be stopped.

Vagina Warriors love to dance.

They are directed by vision, not ruled by ideology.

They are citizens of the world. They cherish humanity over nationhood.

They have a wicked sense of humor. A Palestinian activist told jokes to the Israeli soldier pointing a machine gun at her as she tried to pass the checkpoints. She literally disarmed him with her humor.

They know that compassion is the deepest form of memory.

They know that punishment does not make abusive people behave better. They know that it is more important to provide a space where the best can emerge rather than "teaching people a lesson." I met an extraordinary activist in San Francisco, a former prostitute who had been abused as a child. Working with the correctional system, she devised a therapeutic workshop where convicted pimps and johns could confront their loneliness, insecurity, and sorrow.

Vagina Warriors are done being victims. They know

no one is coming to rescue them. They would not want to be rescued.

They have experienced their rage, depression, desire for revenge, and they have transformed them through grieving and service. They have confronted the depth of their darkness.

They live in their bodies.

They are community makers. They bring everyone in.

They have a keen ability to live with ambiguity. They can hold two opposite thoughts at the same time. I first recognized this quality during the Bosnian war. I was in a refugee camp interviewing a Muslim woman activist whose husband had been decapitated by a Serb. I asked her if she hated Serbs. She looked at me as if I were crazy. "No, no, I do not hate Serbs," she said. "If I were to hate Serbs, then the Serbs would have won."

Vagina Warriors know that the process of healing from violence is long and happens in stages. They *give* what they *need* the most, and by giving this they heal and activate the wounded part inside.

For native people, a warrior is one whose basic responsibility is to protect and preserve life. The struggle to end violence on this planet is a battle. Emotional, intellectual, spiritual, physical. It requires every bit of our strength, our courage, our fierceness. It means speaking out when everyone says to be quiet. It means going the distance to hold perpetrators accountable for their actions. It means honoring the truth even if it means losing family, country, and friends. It means developing the muscle to survive the grief that violence brings and entering a dangerous space of stunned unknowing.

Like vaginas, these warriors are central to human existence, but they still remain largely unvalued and unseen. In every community there are humble activists working every day to undo suffering. They sit by hospital beds, pass new laws, chant taboo words, write boring proposals, beg for money, demonstrate and hold vigils in the streets. They are our mothers, our daughters, our sisters, our aunts, our grandmothers, and our best friends.

Many Vagina Warriors work primarily on a grassroots level. Because what is done to women is often done in isolation and remains unreported, Vagina Warriors work to make the invisible seen. Mary, in Chicago, fights for the rights of women of color so that they are not disregarded or abused; Nighat risked stoning and public shaming in Pakistan by producing *The Vagina Monologues* in Islamabad so that the stories and passions of women would not go unheard. Esther Chávez Cano has worked for years to stop the murders and mutilations of the women in Ciudad Juárez. Originally she had gone there to take care of an ailing aunt for what she thought would be a few months. But the stories of the murdered and violated young women began to occupy her. Before she knew it, she was dedicating her life to their safety and protection. Esther was a recently retired executive accountant. At an age when she could have finally felt secure, she moved herself from a luxurious and comfortable lifestyle in Mexico City to a life of ongoing threats, dangerous nights, and constant stress. In 1998 she opened Casa Amiga, a center for the battered, raped, and missing women of Ciudad Juárez.

A WORLD OF BRENDAS

As we landed in El Paso, Texas, the turbulence in the airplane was the kind that made you inappropriately squeeze the hand of a business associate. We were en route to Ciudad Juárez, Mexico. The sky was liquid mud—murky, windy, and dangerous. It was as if something terrible were about to happen.

This, it turns out, was the ongoing state in Ciudad Juárez. In the past ten years more than four hundred women have disappeared from this border zone between the U.S. and Mexico. Three hundred seventy have turned up murdered, mutilated, tortured, and raped.

Within minutes outside the airport, my teeth were crunching dust, which tasted like bone. In so many of the stories of the atrocities that happened here, the women end up as bone.

The first thing Esther Chávez Cano told me as we drove toward Ciudad Juárez was that a mother recently went to identify her disappeared brown-haired daughter in a morgue. It turned out the girl they had found had red hair, but the authorities had dyed her hair black, hoping they would be able to fool her mother. Of course her mother was able to quickly see through the terrible dye job done to the corpse.

"This is what the Mexican authorities do now," Esther told me. "Rather than finding the killers or convicting them, they try to change the identity of the dead, hoping to trick the relatives. Obviously it has nothing to do with making Ciudad Juárez safer for women or bringing brutal murderers and rapists to justice. It has to do with getting the families of the dead off their backs."

Esther told me all this as we drove across the U.S. border into Mexico. We had hardly said hello. But this was what Esther was thinking about. There was really nothing else on her mind. Small talk would have seemed absurd and insulting. I noticed as we sped over the border into Mexico that we did not get stopped. There was no one even in the security booth, no one checking passports. The last time I had returned from Ciudad Juárez, it took almost three hours to get across the border, as the search and security was so high going into the United States. I wondered why no one cared who went into Ciudad Juárez. But unfortunately, I knew the answer.

Esther told me that El Paso had become a kind of dumping ground for rapists from all over the U.S. There were something like 716 convicted rapists living in El Paso, and any one of them could easily get over the border.

Everything about Ciudad Juárez was unsettling. It was a place, as one woman told me, that no one chose to live in, a border state that didn't really exist on the human map. The majority of those who lived here had fallen through the cracks and were suspended endlessly in a state of hunger, terror, and longing. El Paso, a booming metropolis with tall buildings, was so close you could touch it, forever reminding the poor that dreams did come true for the deserving, which they were not.

Ciudad Juárez was like an exhausted prostitute, endlessly used. It got used by the multinationals that have built their maquiladoras (factories owned primarily by U.S.-based companies), where they paid thousands of workers, mainly women, less than six dollars a day for nine hours of work. It got used by drug dealers, who bought and sold with no consequences. It got used by pimps and johns, who abducted, sold, raped, brutalized, and mutilated women with impunity.

No one planned to stay in Ciudad Juárez. It felt like everyone was passing through, although many had accidentally ended up there for life. Nothing was secure or safe. Houses of the poor were made of paper and tires. One shack I visited housed six adults and four children. There were two small beds and a hot plate, and the dust blew in so intensely and regularly that the mother of the house spent most of her day just sweeping it out so they could try to breathe at night.

Ciudad Juárez reminded me of war zones I have visited. The same existential landscape of broken nothingness, the same sense of danger, the same remnants of terrible violence. The same dark despair that settled into your bones with the dust. That dust, again, that dust. A dust that was produced not only by war on the property and people of this world but by the relentless war on the souls of the poor.

There were also the survivors, women who through sheer creative will and humor somehow kept the community intact. Esther nurtured these women and fought for them.

In front of Casa Amiga, on a fairly dangerous street, was a tree that was mainly stumps. It had nails sticking out from all its limbs and trunk. To me this tree represented everything about the women of Ciudad Juárez: still living somehow, still growing in totally dangerous soil in spite of having been maimed and violated. Casa Amiga was a center for the battered, the raped, and the mothers of the murdered. It was a center of stories and nightmares and resistance.

The first story I heard was about a young woman named Brenda. The next story I heard was about a young woman named Brenda. They were different women, and their stories do not end the same way, but I realized very quickly that Ciudad Juárez was a world of Brendas. They were young, brown, pretty, and very poor. They had become as disposable as empty Coca-Cola cans. Sometimes their bones turned up next to old bottles in parking lots. Sometimes their bodies were never found. Sometimes they were blamed for being mutilated and tortured because of what they'd been wearing. They were rapidly becoming an endangered species.

I got up at 5 A.M. to meet Brenda, who was nineteen. Every morning for the last two years she had walked down this dark, pothole-filled road to a darker corner to wait for a bus that would take her to her job at the maquiladora. It was cold at that time of morning, very cold. The roosters crowed, her dog barked madly outside her house, but they had not protected her and they would not protect her now if she was alone. Since she had been attacked and almost murdered two months earlier, her mother, Silvia, a devout Christian, walked with her many mornings to the bus stop.

Several years before, Brenda had gone to apply for a job. There was a long line of pretty, thin ladies. She started dieting and quickly became bulimic, believing that people only value you by the way you look. When she was seventeen, after she lost a great deal of weight, she went into a maquiladora and challenged the woman hiring to give her a chance to prove herself. Her boss bragged to me that Brenda was "a really good worker, although she has not been the same since the attack. She is quiet now. She is reserved, not so confident. And she has lost almost sixty pounds. She is still a good worker though."

On the day of her attack, Brenda had $160 in her pockets that her friends had all saved for her to buy clothes. She had stayed late at the factory for therapy, as she was trying to manage her bulimia. When she came out of the factory she remembered saying good-bye to the man who sold candies. She went to the public phone, called her mother to say she was coming home. Her brother said her mother was already on the way to pick her up. Her back was to the street. Her arms were crossed. Suddenly she felt someone grab her. She hadn't heard a car drive up. They tore off her backpack. They threw her into a car facedown on the floor.

There were three men, two in the front, one in the back. The guy in the back pulled out a gun.

"I remember I was wearing Band-Aids from where the machines at work hurt my hands. The guy asked me, 'Do you want to die? Look at her wrists. She wants to die.' I said, 'No, you motherfucker, I do not want to die.' He slapped my face. He threw me on the floor again. He covered my eyes with cloth. He told me over and over not to look at him or he would kill me. He started taking things out of the bag. All my money, all hundred and sixty dollars. I had a notebook filled with homework that the psychologist told me to do. He started making fun of my homework. It was about my dreams for the future. Then there were things I had written about food and being bulimic. He told me he was going to kill me 'cause my life was so fucked up. He found my work card. He asked me if I was really nineteen. He asked if I knew what having a man was. I said I doubted there was a man in the car. I don't know how I said this. They beat me more. They kept me in the car for two hours riding and riding around. They said I made more noise than the others. I didn't know what they meant, but I could see this pocketbook of another girl on the floor. I wondered what they did to her. I was very angry. I thought I wouldn't be getting out of the car so I'd have to fight. They stopped and got drugs. They were inhaling cocaine, getting crazier and crazier, smoking, dropping ashes on my legs. They touched me sexually. I scratched one of them. He hit me again. They were all hitting me. People say in those moments your whole life flashes before your eyes and you think about your family. I didn't think about my family. I thought about how angry I was. One of the guys told me he liked how aggressive I was, he liked how I answered. They kept hurting me. It went on forever. Then suddenly they got sick of me. They talked about need-ing to find a new girl and threw me out of the car."

Brenda's mother, Silvia, called Esther Chávez when Brenda got home, and Esther came right over. Brenda was a mess: her face was beaten and swollen, and her clothes were completely bloody. "At the beginning I to-tally blamed myself for what I was wearing," Brenda said, "but Esther told me it doesn't matter what you're wearing. No one has the right to do this to you."

"I'm shy now," Brenda said. "I've lost my confi-dence. I am always aware in the streets, always looking around. I have much more trouble trusting people." Silvia told me that the biggest change in Brenda was that she'd stopped going to church. "She used to like church. Now she refuses to go. My girls are good. It is hard to believe something like this can happen to someone who is good. My girls don't go dancing. I know there is danger everywhere. Every day when I go out I am afraid. Particularly when I go with Brenda to the factory. I never show Brenda I am afraid. For me the most important thing is that Brenda believes in God."

I asked her what she wanted to do to the men who did this to her daughter. She said, "I pray for them. I have been praying to stop evil and for them to stop these crimes and ask God to take care of the girls in this city."

I noticed that Brenda wore three rubber bands on her wrist. "My therapist told me to wear them," she said. "I have so many negative thoughts. The word always repeats and repeats in my head. Something always bad will happen. You will always be afraid. My therapist told me to snap my wrists with the rubber bands when my brains start to talk like this. The rubber bands hurt and it stops for a while."

She told me she didn't want to tell anyone at the beginning but Esther helped her. She thought of those guys in the car saying they needed to find another girl, and this gave her the strength to speak out.

"I hope me telling this will help them," she said quietly.

Esther Luna was forty-six. She was beautiful, humble, gentle, and intense. The first thing she showed us was the portrait of herself and her three daughters. They all looked strangely terrorized and detached. One daughter, Brenda, who was five in the picture, was making a funny twisted face. It was as if she were anticipating her future.

Esther told me they used to have a normal life until the violence came to the city. Well, normal like the "normal" life of living with a violent, alcoholic husband. They had lots of troubles. He terrorized and abused the four children for years. Then he kicked all of them out. They had no money, nowhere to go. Esther Luna got a job as a domestic worker, but she couldn't pay the rent. Brenda Luna was fifteen. She suggested that her mother get a second job and let her take her job as a domestic worker. Esther Luna was reluctant but desperate. The day before Brenda was to begin the job, her mother took her to the bus stop and walked her through the not-too-complicated route to the job. Brenda left the next morning and never returned that evening. At first Esther Luna thought she was with friends, but when the morning came and Brenda was still not there, she became worried. She got on the bus and went to the home where Brenda was supposed to have been headed the day before. Her boss told Esther that her daughter had never been there. Esther Luna was panicked. Her boss brought her to the police. This began the torturous search for her daughter.

Three weeks later a body was found and Esther Luna was summoned to the police station. Most of the found body was bone except for several places where flesh remained. On the left calf, Esther Luna was able to identify a scar where a dog had bitten her daughter when she was a child. She also was able to identify the clothing that was found next to her body. They were definitely Brenda's panties and bra.

The authorities didn't believe her. They said a scar wasn't enough to identify a body. They did a DNA test. One year later they came and told her it wasn't her daughter. Esther told me she knew it was her daughter when she was standing next to the body. "There was something in my heart. I touched the body. I wasn't re-pulsed. I just felt this pain. They found a knife inside her body, where her stomach once was.

"I wanted answers. I made them do another DNA test. I made them test another part of the body, another bone. Another year passed and then they came and told me they lost the tests. I demanded another test. They started to get angry with me. They said this is not your daughter's body. Everyone knew me at the police. They told me my daughter was on the streets crazy with a man. They said terrible things. I told them I didn't care if she was with a man on the streets. I wanted her alive no matter what she was doing. They made fun of me. I stopped going to them because I was humiliated.

"Then I found Casa Amiga. Esther Chávez helped me get a lawyer and they did the first real DNA test and it turned out that it was my daughter. It took almost five and a half years to find out it was my daughter. It took me all those years to find out what I already knew."

She told me about Brenda Luna.

"She was a very happy girl. She told a lot of jokes. She spoke loud. She used to cheer me up. She used to stand behind her brother and sisters and make faces. They gave me a body, but they didn't tell me who did this to my daughter. I want them to investigate. I think they are very powerful people to rape these girls and sell their organs. They must look good, respectable, to get the confidence of the girls. Brenda didn't trust people. They know what they are doing."

We sat in silence. I asked her if she'd been to Brenda's grave.

She told me no buses went there. She didn't have a car. It was in the desert. I told her I would take her there. It was the first time she was happy.

The next day we drove out into the desert. It was hot, dusty, lonely desert. We came to San Rafael: hundreds of crosses that suddenly appeared out of the miles and miles of sand. In the parking lot they sold flowers and wreaths. Esther Luna knew exactly what she wanted for her daughter's grave. White flowers because they were pure and a wreath with the guardian angel. "My children," she said, "always pray to the guardian angel that takes care of children whenever they are in trouble."

The graveyard stretched out for miles. Esther Luna had a tiny piece of worn paper with directions: a series of penciled cross marks and then one with a circle around it and the name Brendita. There were thousands of poor people's graves. We narrowed it down to the Patio de Niños. We spread out, a group of us searching for the grave of Brenda Luna. It was hot. There were so many graves, and they all looked the same. Even now Esther Luna could not find her daughter. Miraculously one of us came upon Brenda's grave. Her name had been almost fully bleached off the white

wooden cross. Esther Luna, this quiet, humble, intro-
verted woman, made a beeline for the grave and without pause or ceremony threw herself facedown on her
daughter's desert mound. She covered Brenda Luna's
body with her body. She held her daughter there like
she once held her as a child. She lay there facedown;
her arms pulled at the sand in a swimming motion; her
hands gathered back the dirt on the grave as if she were
reassembling her daughter's mutilated body. She spoke
to her daughter as she lay there, caressing and swimming and gathering.

"Those dogs, those dogs who ripped you apart, my
Brenda." She sobbed, wailed, called out to the Virgin
Mary, who she was sure knew her suffering, having lost
her only child. "You must have needed another angel
to help you. You must have needed my angel."

She kissed the grave over and over.

Then after quite some time she got up, and with
total purpose, she ritualistically decorated the grave
with flowers and wreaths as if she were dressing her
daughter for her *quinceañera* (a coming-out party for
fifteen-year-old girls). At times you could actually see
Esther Luna brushing her daughter's hair. She asked
her seven-year-old son to collect stones to make a circle
around the grave. She laid the stones like jewels. She
watered the grave with her hands dipped into a bucket
and carefully covered every inch of the dry grave as if
she were lotioning her daughter's parched skin. She

said over and over, "Oh my dear daughter. You were so thirsty." She purified her daughter. She paid the men who worked in the graveyard one hundred pesos to paint her daughter's name, Brenda Luna, and her age, fifteen *años*, on her cross, in black.

Even now in 2006, after years of rallies, ongoing struggle from local women's groups, pressure from international organizations, legal cases filed, thousands of people writing and marching in the streets, the Mexican government and the U.S. multinationals that benefit from women working at slave wages still have not moved to protect Mexican women.

Esther Luna was able to find her daughter in miles of barely marked graves in a desolate desert. But the people in power in the local and national Mexican government haven't been able to find or convict one single murderer in ten years.

Poor people, particularly women, create something out of nothing over and over. With stones and a plastic bucket of water and some flowers, Esther Luna honored Brenda and made her sacred. The impoverished emptiness of her grave was transformed. The superwealthy executives who own the maquiladoras can't, in many cases, find the will or resources even to secure a simple streetlight outside the factories so women don't have to walk home in the dark.

THE MEMORY OF HER FACE:
CIUDAD JUÁREZ

Each woman is dark, particular, young.

Each woman has brown eyes, each woman is gone.

There is one girl missing for ten months.

She was seventeen when they took her away

She worked in the maquiladora

She stamped thousands of coupons of products

She would never afford

Four dollars a day

They paid her and bused her to the desert

To sleep in freezing shit

It must have been on the way to the bus

They took her

It must have been dark outside

It must have lasted until morning

Whatever they did to her

It went on and on

You can tell from the others

Who showed up without hands or nipples
It must have gone on and on,
When she finally reappeared
She was bone
Bone bone
No cute mole above her right eye, no
Naughty smile, no wavy black hair.

Bone she came back as bone
She and the others
All beautiful
All beginning
All coupons
All faces
All gone
300 faces gone
300 noses
300 chins
300 dark penetrating eyes
300 smiles
300 mulatto-colored cheeks
300 hungry mouths
About to speak
About to tell
About to scream
Gone
Now
Bone.

I tried to turn away
When they raised the plastic cloth
That concealed
The bone outline of her head
In the morgue
I tried to turn away.

WAITING FOR MR. ALLIGATOR

Until recently, I believed that waiting was a form of protection, a state that ensured my ultimate security. Until recently, I was always waiting for something. I did not know who or what it was, but it hung there, this possibility, this thing on the edge of my mind. I had been waiting for so long it had simply become what I did. Sometimes it was conscious, but most of the time it was like a reflex, a verb that was my verb: waiting.

I think it is why I felt so connected to refugees, homeless women, women in prison. They spent their lives waiting—waiting for a return to their homeland, waiting for a new country to invite them in, waiting for a place where they can finally undo their bags, waiting for escape.

It is why I loved mail. I loved opening the mailbox. I loved sealed envelopes. I loved going through the pile and seeing some handwriting I didn't recognize. There,

there. It might be there. It might be in that letter. I was always thinking today it would arrive. I would open the envelope. It would be inside.

When I was drinking and drugging, it was the next ice-clinking gin and tonic, the next hit of white powdered methedrine. When I was wild and promiscuous, it was the next man or woman I could strip off my clothes with, the next person with whom I could go all the way. But all the way where?

At various times I imagined this thing would come as a trophy, an announcement, an invitation. Once I almost caught it deep in the center of the gentlest, hungriest kiss.

This waiting was a very specific feeling. I remember, on Christmas mornings (which were often fraught, because of my father's radical mood swings), insanely unwrapping my presents even though we were supposed to do the unwrapping in a modulated, thoughtful way. I remember thinking, this one will be it. This shiny or fuzzy or brand-new thing in this endless tissue paper will be what I am waiting for.

I remembered once being in a forest and getting lost and being worried and sitting down and my pants got wet and then finding this fiddlehead fern. This perfect green wrapped piece of life that would unfurl and become something grand, something beautiful. Whatever it was that I was waiting for would be like that: green and becoming bigger than itself.

There were people who were not waiting for anything. I knew some of these people. Somehow, either
they got this thing early on, or they were perfectly
happy living with the absence of it. Their verb was different. They were living, discovering, being, experienc-
ing, getting lost. They were not after anything. They
were not waiting.

I spent way too many hours psychoanalyzing this
preoccupation. What was it I missed? What early psychological wound created such longing? What was I
overcompensating for, trying to fix or to fill? My
mother's absence, my father's cruelty. Blah blah blah.

Sometimes I think that it was just some hole, some
existential yawn inside my being, a muscular craving
for some part of myself that got unhinged at birth.

Or maybe it was the repository wound, the accu-
mulation of the multitudes of losses throughout many
lifetimes—the betrayals, the deaths, the regrets. A kind
of active and ancient graveyard in my psyche.

Or was this waiting a residue memory of another
world inside this world? Was it a desire to evoke a world
I once knew, remember a place I called home, an alternative paradigm that lives parallel to this paradigm?

Maybe the waiting was some deluded fantasy or the
kind of insane optimism that masks deep despair that
there is something or someone coming to make sense
of this, to make it better. Maybe I was simply unable to
face the profound pointlessness of this whole existence.

So instead, I waited. There was a future in waiting.

And what would happen if this thing were to finally arrive, and I were to get what I was waiting for? Would I just die? Would I finally be safe, secure? Would I have a center, a place, a reason for being?

As a teenager I found objects that became the symbols, the projections, of this thing I was waiting for. When I was fifteen and sixteen, it was butterflies. I drew them. I dreamed about them. I studied them. I wrote poems about them. Each time one would appear near me, it was proof of the presence of something mystical, something arriving. When I was seventeen and eighteen, it was a leather hippie headband with a strip of purple suede. When I had it tied around my forehead, it was a magnet, drawing this thing, this possible future, to me.

But the truth is, this waiting started much earlier. It started in darkness, in terror. It started inside the drunk and dangerous voice of my father threatening to annihilate me. It started in his hard, hateful hand on the side of my little face, in the cold indifference of his eyes, in the shaking rage of his pursed lips. It started in my room after a beating, after his belt had made swollen welts on my legs. After he had banged my teenage head over and over against the wood paneling on the den wall, after the blood poured from my nose on the white-and-red checkered tablecloth in the family restaurant and I was rushed to the bathroom to stop the

bleeding, so I wouldn't make him feel bad by reminding him he had punched me. It started in my room,
alone. After the punching and whipping and screaming
had stopped and there was only the buzzing in my
head and the exhaustion from the crashing adrenaline
rush and the guilt and the embarrassment. It started in
that bleakness, that incessant rocking on my bed. Waiting was better than cutting myself or making myself
bleed. Waiting was better than murdering my father or
imagining his electrocution. Waiting was less dangerous than killing. I did not want to be a killer. I was
afraid to be a killer. So I learned how to wait.

As my situation got more desperate, I could no longer
wait for something broad and abstract. So I invented a
being that was coming to get me. The being could not
be human. I did not trust humans. The being was not
really benevolent or cuddly. I had no use for soft and
cuddly. I was always wary that inside that which appeared to be tender was something cruel.

I was waiting for Mr. Alligator. He was a little man-
reptile. He had an alligator body and short human legs.
He was friendly to children in need. He existed for
them. He was on call. He protected them. He was only
dangerous to perpetrators—he could easily devour the
scariest corporate daddy. He had a special phone number you could only access if you were in trouble. When
I came to a certain level of desperation, I would suddenly remember it. I would call him. I would speak to

him loudly as if there were a bad connection. My father and my family would know that Mr. Alligator was on the phone, know there was someone out there listening, watching, witnessing.

"Hi, Mr. Alligator," I would say. "It's me, Evie." (They called me Evie then.) "It's Evie and I need you to come and get me. I need you to come as soon as you can. It is bad here. They are mean to me. They do not love me. But I know you love me. So please, when can you come, Mr. Alligator? Please can you come soon?"

He would promise to get there as soon as possible. I knew he was busy. There were other children calling. I knew because once after my father had thrown me against a wall, I had tried to call him and his line was busy.

After he and I had spoken, I would go to my room and pack this little brown suitcase. I would put in it my pocketbook-size hairbrush, three Magic Markers (always a purple), and some cookies. I would leave the house. I would walk down the path on our front lawn and I would sit at the end of it, my sneakers compulsively rubbing the gravel in the driveway.

I would wait for him. Sometimes I would wait an hour, sometimes the whole day. The waiting became my defiance. I could not be deterred. My mother would come out after I missed a meal and tell me to come inside, to stop with the nonsense. But this was not nonsense to me. This was as serious as life and death. Mr.

Alligator was coming. He was the future. He was mine, something I was creating, dreaming. He loved me. He was going to make everything better. He had to. There was no other way I could go on.

Of course he never did show up.

Well, that is not exactly true. Forty years later, I went to Africa because I had heard there were women who were working to stop the practice of female genital mutilation. Agnes Pareiyo was one of them. She lived in the Rift Valley. One day when she was twelve, she was taken against her will and brought into a dark room. Two women held her down and an older woman cut off her clitoris with a razor. She wasn't allowed to scream or make a noise because it would mean she was weak.

After they mutilated her she was forced to lie still with her legs tied together for three days. They forced her to clean her wound by peeing on herself. The pain was unimaginable. She would try not to scream. This unexpressed scream has lived in her bones to this day.

Agnes was never the same again. The cutting took her clitoris. She never knew sexual pleasure again. She was forced to give up something essential, against her will. Her whole community was involved in this undertaking, so it robbed her trust.

When she grew up, Agnes could not bear the idea of this happening to other little girls. So she set out with a magic box that contained a woman's medical torso. It had a vagina and vagina replacement parts. She walked through the dusty Rift Valley from community to community. The Masai are essentially nomadic, so she would travel hours, days, before she found a family or tribe. She taught mothers and fathers and girls and boys what a healthy vagina looked like and what a mutilated vagina looked like. She showed them the various forms of mutilation and the way the vagina got sewn back together after being cut, sometimes with thorns. She showed them the dangers of cutting—the risk of infection, AIDS, and dying from painful childbirth. She taught young boys about how their wives would never know pleasure so the love between them would be void and empty. She showed young girls how, if they saved their clitoris, they would get to go to school and would not be forced into marriage at a very young age with a very old man. She created an alternative ritual for girls that celebrated their coming-of-age with dance and music and theater. The girls received cows as presents, instead of being cut.

Agnes walked through the Rift Valley. She walked for days, for years—from one Masai village to another. Often she slept on the ground. In the years she walked, she saved fifteen hundred girls from being cut.

I asked Agnes what V-Day could do for her, how we could support her. She said, "Eve, if V-Day buys me a jeep, I could get around a lot faster." We bought her a jeep. The first year she had it, she was able to reach forty-five hundred girls. So I asked what else V-Day could do for her. She said, "Eve, if you gave me money, I could build a house for girls so that when they were about to be cut they could run away to the house and save their clitoris and go to school." So we gave her money to build a house.

Two years ago I went back to Africa. There, in the middle of the Rift Valley, was a sign that read TASARU NTOMOMOK RESCUE CENTER FOR THE SCHOOLS—UNTIL THE VIOLENCE STOPS, which is V-Day's slogan.

Agnes had been preparing for this day for weeks. As I drove up I saw hundreds of girls dressed in red (the color of the Masai and also the color of V-Day). I was so overwhelmed I couldn't get out of the jeep. It was a bright sunny African day with a blue blue sky. Finally, my legs wobbly, I climbed out. Agnes greeted me and began to walk me down a path. Suddenly it was the path of my childhood, down the front lawn to the place where I would sit by the road and wait. Now there were girls—young girls, teenage girls—lining the path on either side of me, dancing, stamping the dust, singing a song in Swahili about how the time of female genital mutilation had ended. They gathered around me and dressed me in a red Masai shawl covered with beads and glittering ornaments. Their song, their joy, carried me down the path. There at the end was a house, our house: the V-Day Safe House for Girls. I stood there and realized I wasn't waiting anymore. I was dancing. I was crying. I was singing. I was laughing. But I was not waiting. It had taken almost forty-two years, but Mr. Alligator had finally come. We get rescued by giving what we need the most. What we are waiting for has always lived inside us.

THE SCARIEST THING ABOUT PRISON
WAS NOT THE SPIKED BARBED WIRE

In 1994 I was invited to Bedford Hills Correctional Facility to write a movie about women in prison. I was anxious. My life was dedicated to ending violence. I had spent hours and hours listening to survivors of atrocities. Somehow this violence had become familiar. As awful as the stories were, I identified—or should I say, I only allowed myself to identify—with the people who had suffered and the ways they had suffered.

I had never spent time with the people who had actually perpetrated those violations. I had never sat with murderers. Because of my own history, those rapists and killers and violators were dead to me. They did not have faces. They were deeds, awful deeds. I had built hard walls in myself to keep those criminals locked up, locked away. These internal walls mirrored the literal walls of prison.

And yet I was drawn to Bedford Hills. Again, what I

cannot see has always terrified me and attracted me the most.

Looking back, I have to say the scariest thing about prison was not the electrical gates banging closed behind me on entrance. Not the rolls and rolls of spiked barbed wire surrounding the place. Not the concrete slabs of emptiness that held it up. Not the room full of women dressed in drab green, many of whom had murdered someone or been part of a heinous crime.

The scariest part of prison was falling in love with the women, the inmates in my group. They were smart and funny and beautiful and deeply kind and remorseful and in so much pain, and these same women had killed people, taken actual lives. This complexity, this ambiguity, was almost unbearable. It made me want to flee the prison. Everything was suddenly in question.

I had expected these women to be hard, indifferent, uncaring. They were the enemy. They were violent and immoral and cruel. I was good. I was victimized. I was pure. Suddenly none of this was true. These women were desperately guilty. They hated themselves for what they'd done. They were loving mothers, devoted daughters, generous wives. They were desperate for education, for tools to understand how their lives had gone so wrong, hungry for the resources to make their lives better.

Everyone at Bedford Hills Correctional Facility is there because of a mistake. Some of those mistakes occurred within months—some within minutes. Most of the mistakes were dreadful, catastrophic. Now we have frozen each woman in her mistake. Marked her forever. Held her captive. Discarded. Hated for her mistake. She has essentially been forced to become her mistake, the walking daily embodiment of her mistake. Held in the monument constructed to punishing mistakes.

Before I came to Bedford, I imagined the women there: mistakes lying on mistake cots behind steel mistake bars.

Mistakes do not have faces or feelings or histories or futures. They are bad. Mistakes. We must forget them, put them away.

Then I came to Bedford.

Slowly I began to meet the mistakes, one by one. They had soft, delicate voices, strong hands, beautiful faces, feisty spirits, outrageous laughs. These mistakes were mothers, daughters, sisters, aunts, Christians, Muslims, Buddhists, Jews—they had fantasies and toothaches and bad moods and funky T-shirts.

Then we began our writing group. Twelve different mistakes in one room. I began to see how it worked:

There was the mistake and the woman.

There was the mistake and the woman who got Kleenex any time anyone came close to crying.

There was the mistake and the great deep love of one's child.

The mistake and a brilliant poetic mind.

The mistake and the woman who teaches, who writes, who sings, who braids, who hates herself for her mistake.

There is the mistake and the woman who waits to move on from the mistake, who is desperate for the tools to transform the self that made the mistake, who longs to be seen, to be seen as something other than a mistake.

In our group, I watched women struggle week after week to give words, to give voice to the guilt, the sorrow, the fear, the despair, that had formed around their crimes.

I was honored and—I mean this—privileged to experience the depth of their seeking and reflection. I was moved and changed by their courage and willingness to take full responsibility for their lives and deeds.

There is the mistake. It is one moment. It is in the past. It cannot be changed.

Then there is the woman.

I began with one group of fifteen women. They were all long-termers; most were there for violent crimes. I was there to hear their stories as the basis for the film I was going to write. We met for three hours each week. The first week each woman told her story from ages one to seven, then the next week from ages seven to fourteen, on and on until we got to the woman's crime.

During our first meeting, I immediately became engaged and connected with every woman except one. This woman was there for a terrible crime. A crime for which, because of my own history, I had no compassion or forgiveness. She had molested children and ended up murdering one of them. I couldn't even look at her. She disgusted me. She had terrible skin and I wished she wasn't in the group. Many of the women in the group had been raped or molested as children, so they despised her as much as I did.

In the second meeting, she sat down right next to me. I wanted to move my seat. I wanted her to go away. I didn't want to know anything about her. I prayed she wouldn't talk. But she did. I tried not to listen. But I was the facilitator of the group. I was there to encourage women to tell their stories. I had to pretend to be interested.

In the telling of her story, my life became uprooted. My security was, until then, based on defining people and myself in neat and organizable constructs. Republican. Conservative. Sexist. Capitalist. Child Molester. It made it easier. Then they could be categorized, judged, and dismissed. This scary woman with the bad skin was a tornado. I felt suddenly like Dorothy falling through space, and my well-constructed house was spinning with me. It was not going to protect me.

It turned out that this woman had been molested from the time she was five years old by her mother and her stepfather. When she was nine they sold her out as a sex toy to willing buyers and neighbors. Men raped her, tied her to beds, and shoved all kinds of objects inside her. When she was fourteen, her mother died. When she was fifteen, her stepfather married her and forced her to work as his assistant pedophile, bringing in children from the neighborhood that they would then molest together. In the course of one of these terrible episodes, a child died.

When she came to prison, she had no idea why she had been arrested. No one had ever provided her with a moral framework or a vision that child molestation was wrong. She had been turned into an object when she was little. She assumed this is what happened to everyone. It took her five years in prison to understand what she had done wrong. Then she began to cut herself on a regular basis.

I sat there as she told her story out loud to a group of women she knew were hating her for what she had done. I sat there as my judgments turned into pain and confusion, and then tears. How can you judge people when you have no idea where they come from?

———

This initial group met about five times. When it was over, I signed on for more. I needed to go deeper. I needed to know more. I committed myself to facilitating a writing group for twelve to fifteen women. It met once a week for three hours. I thought I would do it for a few months. The group lasted for eight years.

Each week I witnessed the women wrestle with the truth, struggling openly with their demons and their culpability. They did not sentimentalize or romanticize their acts. They rarely indulged in self-pity. They worked to be accurate. Often they were merciless with themselves. To be witness to women willing to face the darkest aspect of their own souls and deeds; to see them struggle with their own hand in murder, their own selfishness, their own stupidity, their own rage, their own awful history, their own refusal to be responsible, their own sense of personal and political helplessness, their own despair and suicidal pain, their own fear that there would never be forgiveness, that they had forfeited the right to be; to sit with them in that sea of darkness, that sea of fraught and fierce reckoning, taught me about insecurity.

There were days, too, when I had to struggle with my own judgments, my own feelings about what the women had done. As a woman wept over having stabbed a man twenty-two times to death, I sat there, feeling with her the madness of her sorrow and simultaneously feeling my outrage and horror at her crime.

I had to reckon not only with my terrible judgments but with the parts of me that identified with these women, with the parts of me that were capable of committing such crimes. It was so much easier to characterize them as criminals, to make them hard matter, separate from me, than to realize how truly easy it is for any of us, given certain circumstances, to step over the line. I wanted there to be rules, boundaries. Crazy people do crimes. Mean people do crimes. Bad people do crimes.

One night we were in a basement classroom and the women were reading their writing exercises out loud. They had been asked to write a rant or speech or letter to someone or some institution they felt had wronged them. Some wrote to their parents, some wrote to the government, some wrote to their ex-lovers. They were reading these rants with great passion and, sometimes, great anger. Somewhere in the middle of the evening, it occurred to me that there I was, all alone in a basement with a group of thieves, drug dealers, and murderers venting their rage and passion. And I had never felt safer. Danger lurks when people are dissociated and detached from their own story or feelings. We were together in the center of their story, in the torrent of their feelings, in the truth of their reality. Naked there, exposed there. If there is any security in this world, it is there.

I am not saying people shouldn't be held accountable for terrible acts. But holding people in prisons does not necessarily make them responsible or accountable. It makes them bad. It makes them evil. It puts an end to any process of transformation. It hardens them spiritually and psychologically. But if there are no processes or programs through which people inside can take responsibility for their crimes, admit their guilt, look at what led them to commit those crimes, and release their sorrow and suffering, there is no possibility of change. Not for the prisoners or their victims.

I question deeply the value of punishment/retaliation. I understand that it serves a momentary emotional function: you hurt me, I hurt you back.

But what does it do to the punisher? When I was younger I dreamed of killing my father. I dreamed of other people killing my father. He was so mean, so violent. But I see now this solution would have forever bonded me to my father. Yes, my father would be gone. I would be more secure for that moment. But the act of killing him would have changed my nature, would have made me much more like my father.

This is not to say I do not believe in holding places. But what we do in those places, the transformation of suffering, is much more interesting to me than the hardening and perpetuating of it. If my father were alive and I was allowed to do anything to him, I would ask that he feel what he did to me, come to know what he did to me, own it, apologize for it, and make reparations. I would ask that he spend his days changing the circumstances that created his behavior. This would mean undoing hypermasculinity and male domination. It would mean my father being brave enough and supported enough to feel his vulnerability and sorrow and inadequacies.

Today the United States has the highest prison population in the world, over 2.1 million people. This is the population of a small country. We lock people up at a rate that is seven to ten times that of any other democracy. We build more and more prisons, rather than addressing the poverty, racism, violence, that are the roots of crime. In our need for security, we fortify against our fear rather than changing the circumstances that created it.

BETTY GALE TYSON IS FREE

I had to be there when Betty Gale Tyson stepped into freedom. I had to see the expression on her face, the energy in her body, when she transitioned out of twenty-five years of captivity, when she walked out of the big house, away from the familiarity of daily abuse and disregard, away from the mindless secure routine of daily counts and electric gates slamming shut, the choiceless world of drab green uniforms and black work boots and scentless state-ordered soap. I had to be there when she left her sisters—some she had mothered and protected, others she had loved on the run. I had to be there as she fell out into the wilderness of freedom, separating her from the walls and barbed-wire boundaries she had come to call home. I wanted to catch her, to surround her, but mainly I wanted to be standing there for her. I wanted to be witness. I wanted those twenty-five years to mean something.

I flew in a prop jet to Rochester, New York, at the

same time Betty Gale Tyson was being driven seven and a half hours from the Bedford Hills Correctional Facility to a Rochester jail. She was about to be released. Her sentence had been vacated because her lawyer had found enough evidence to reveal the illegal procedures surrounding her case.

I was in Rochester because her family had invited me, allowed me into their waiting. They had rented a long white limousine. There in the limo outside the jail I moved in with Betty Gale's history. I sat by her mother, who was attached to an oxygen tank, terrified she would stop breathing before her daughter was free. I sat with her beautiful sisters, who were dressed in high heels and gold. I sat with their longing and missing and resentment and explosive joy.

I had fallen in love with Betty Gale Tyson eight months before at Bedford Hills Correctional Facility. I had met her in the damp underground room where I was running a group for long-termers. There was no sunlight on her face. She was shivering. She was always cold. I offered her my leather jacket. She petted it and moaned over how much she missed leather and longed to wear black. (Wearing black is illegal in prison; only green is allowed.) She made a sound in her throat, like an *mm-hmm,* but it was deeper, more significant, more compelling. She took me with that *mm-hmm.* She took me by surprise. Maybe it was her predicament that made me fall in love with her: twenty-five years in prison for a crime she did not commit because she was severely beaten into a confession by the detective on her case. Betty Gale was twenty-five years old when they put her in prison. She was a drug addict, poor and black, working the streets. They were looking for a murderer. She was available. It did not matter to the police that she was not the murderer. It did not matter because Betty Gale Tyson's life did not matter to them; she was poor, black, and drug-addicted.

Maybe I fell in love with the way she handled her predicament—no bitterness, none, only sadness sometimes and this feeling of always being cold. Maybe it was her beauty, her cheeks, her smile, her waist-long dreadlocks. When she wrapped them on top of her head, she was an Egyptian queen. Maybe it was her name, Betty Gale Tyson. Betty Gale Tyson. You did not forget that name. Maybe it was the way she wore her prison uniform, the skirt short, her legs strong, sculpted, gorgeous. Maybe it was the way she refused to die, refused to give up her passion, her body, her desires, how she kept herself fulfilled and connected and naked and hot for twenty-five years behind bars. Maybe it was how much the other inmates loved her and counted on her and had been changed and helped by her. How she held the sick women and those who were dying of AIDS, and baked carrot cake for the young inmates and taught them patience and gave them presents until they learned the ropes. Maybe I wanted to be like Betty

Gale Tyson. The world had determined her conditions—
as insecure, uncaring, filthy, and cruel as can be—yet
she refused to allow the world to change her nature.

At a little after eight o'clock, Betty Gale walked out
the doors of the jail, dressed in white and high heels.
She was a vision. There was a crowd of people who had
known her, and knew about her case, and they went
crazy. When she finally made her way to the limo, her
family pulled her inside like they were rescuing a
drowning swimmer and dove in unison on top of her.
There was this sound, this guttural collective family cry,
this howl that went on and on.

Later that night we ate cold cuts in a hotel suite. It
was a party. The family was wild with relief as they kept
watching Betty Gale on the TV news. It was their way
of confirming that yes, she was in fact there with them
in the room. Praise the Lord. Betty Gale Tyson was free.

Afterward, I held Betty Gale in my arms and she
cried. Twenty-five years of tears began to fall out of her.
On the same night she got her freedom, she felt so
guilty she cried, not for the crime she hadn't committed, but for the sisters in prison she had left behind.

III

LEAVING
MY FATHER'S
HOUSE

RECKONING

Sometimes in the morning at breakfast after a violent night, my father would lean over and ask me where I had gotten the bruise on my neck. It was always a terribly awkward moment. I would sit for a few minutes. How did I get the bruise on my neck? The question would lie there manically flipping over and over in my brain like a docked trout searching for water. I would consider my options. Tell him the truth—that he had choked me during a drunken rage and had made the bruise. Lie, and say I had fallen. Touch my neck like I was only just discovering it—"What bruise?"

Often my mother was there. She would look at me with that look that begs you not to make trouble. Which says haven't you already done enough, haven't you made our lives miserable by being so intense, so difficult, so defiant. I would ponder deeper. I would take in this morning version of my father—sober, devastatingly handsome, clean and groomed. He smelled good. He was vulnerable the way one is vulnerable the morning after heavy drinking. My father was always vulnerable and full of a terrible melancholy in the morning. This is why I slept late. My father usurped the morning.

I would sit, suspended, unable to answer. To lie would be compromising my integrity, my character. Ironically, it had been my father who taught me this. Lying, to my father, was worse than murdering. Lying would mean denying, pretending, acting as if what happened had not happened, acting as if this violence hadn't occurred at all. But telling the truth risked a worse fate. Telling the truth would mean hurting my father, shaming my father, embarrassing my father, reminding my father. Reminding him of the other person who lived inside him, reminding him he was capable of enormous cruelty, that he was an alcoholic and had no control and became someone else—which is why he couldn't remember the source of the bruise on my neck. The fact that he had beaten me or choked me or almost murdered me the night before was so much less disturbing to me than the idea of undoing my father, demythologizing my father, crushing my father's idea of himself, his masculinity, his power. So inevitably I sacrificed my wholeness—my knowledge and need for the truth—for his security, for his comfort. I understand now that I did this more for my security than for his.

———

I knew, even at that young age, how fragile his identity was. Even though I was little and a girl, I knew that I was stronger than my father. I could not have articulated how or in what way, but I was stronger. My father could crumble and break. My father, like an overstuffed piggy bank, was crammed dangerously full of sorrow, bitterness, and hate. One more penny, one wrong insult or hurt, could burst the bank open and there would be no stopping the breaking into pieces and pieces, there would be no stopping the bleeding. Then there would be no more Daddy. He would die in shame. He would die feeling like nothing. He would die.

I knew that my father, who appeared handsome and strong, was rigged with cardboard and rubber bands. There in the center, where there should be something tangible, was absence. There in the center, which should have been the place connecting the whole story or person, was a dark deep cavern. There was no bridge over this hole. So my father had no memory of the bruise on my neck or how his insane choking hands had actually made the black and blue. We call this dissociation. But it is more profound than that. My father could be funny or brilliant or clever, but really could not be found. My father did not feel what I was feeling when he was beating me, or he would never have beaten me again. Someone else did the beating. Someone he created long ago to survive the pain he was once not allowed to feel.

When he was dying, he made my mother promise not to call me. He did not feel what this would be like for his daughter not to be able to reckon with or touch or say goodbye to her father.

Maybe I was stronger because I had not been trained in the ways of men. I had not yet learned how to disconnect. I was drawn to the fire. As a matter of fact, I hungered for it—it was beautiful, magical, and powerful. I wanted to sit by it. I wanted to get warmed by it. I wanted to burn in it.

My father was no longer brave enough to know the fire. That had been long since beaten and bargained out of him. I had to protect him from the fire, but more important, I had to protect myself from his weakness. He was my father. I needed him to be strong. So I invented him. I made him up.

We do this with fathers and we do this with lovers and husbands and presidents. Rather than removing them or firing them or calling them out, we make excuses for them. We pretend that what they are really doing is not what they are doing. We tell ourselves they mean to be doing something else.

I did not tell myself my father was weak. I told myself he was sensitive. I told myself he was special. I did not tell myself he was indifferent to me. I told myself he loved me too much. I did not tell myself that he was the

person making me unsafe and he could one day murder me. I told myself he was my father, my leader. He
was right. It was my fault. If I could only be more good,
more understanding, he would do right and relax. I did
not tell myself that my father was conscious, that he
had an agenda, that he knew what he was doing, that
he was numb to me and only out for himself, that he
was selfish and narcissistic. Instead, I felt his unfelt sorrow and loneliness. It became my sorrow and loneliness. It occupied me and it became my job to build the
bridge over that cavern in his center. I devoted most of
my life to it. I had a shrink who used to say I pasted on
the arms of my lovers so they could hug me. But unfortunately, when they got arms, they would invariably
hug someone else.

In my mind, I made my father a lonely, sorrowful
man rather than a violent perpetrator. Now, at fifty-
two, there is a reckoning. Now I have had to come to
see that my pasting the arms or building the bridge was
not for him but for me. If my father was lonely and I
could get him to feel it, he would one day possibly feel
something for me. Then I would have a father who
could take care of me. Then I would be someone. I
would not be alone.

Reckoning: You made the bruise, Dad. You choked me
and choked me. And Mom, who had never moved be-

fore during your violent bouts, did this time because I had been gagging and had stopped breathing. She screamed and pulled you off. You almost murdered me. You had no remorse. You never did. You didn't do this because you couldn't tolerate your love for me. You did it because where there is no center, there is brutal indifference.

Reckoning: I cannot make myself less or worse. I am this intense. I am this alive. I am this powerful.

Reckoning: There is no one coming. There is nothing secure. There is only the unveiling.

FREE FALLING

think of the security of cages. How violence, cruelty, oppression, become a kind of home, a familiar pattern, a cage, in which we know how to operate and define ourselves. I think of Betty Gale Tyson leaving the prison after twenty-five years. I think of Cindy Sheehan leaving her marriage and home. I think how incredibly difficult it has been for them to live outside those walls.

Those of us who have been violated or around violence or cruelty—and really those of us who have simply grown up in a racist, sexist, homophobic world— knew how far we could go, how loud we could get, how big we could become, how much space or attention we could occupy. We learned the price we had to pay for our bigness, our desire, and our ambition. We were practiced at the dance. We cherished the walls of our confines because they gave definition to our lives, boundaries. We wrongly believed this was safety, protection. We made sure someone was assigned to bring us down a notch, remind us who we really are, hold the truth of our badness.

My father said I was bad. He called me a whore, a jackass, an idiot. He was never—and I mean never—wrong.

I believed my story up until a year ago. I was contained by this story. Defined by it. I knew who I was. I could drive the highway of my self-hatred with my eyes closed. It was that familiar, and I often mistook familiarity for security. I was allowed to be successful, big in the world, important on the outside, if I agreed to be wrong, selfish, bad on the inside. I truly believed this was the only way I could operate in the world. I was terrified that if I were to go out there, outside the confines of this self-imposed prison, someone would actually kill me. But more important, I was terrified that I would hurt my father with my life force, burn him with my light, my creativity, my love of people, and my lack of fear of them. I was terrified I would leave him behind and he would be humiliated and lost.

In 2004, I was ready to leave, jump off the cliff, and be alone: free fall. I think that being post-fifty had something to do with it, or doing ashtanga yoga and feeling strong in my body, or performing a play about being good and realizing it was up to me to decide if I *was* good. I could not let anyone else make such a decision anymore. I had assigned this role to my partners.

As with my father, if they determined I was bad, they had control over me. Because what I wanted most was to be good. As long as the carrot dangled in front of me, as long as they might one day say it, know it, feel it, I had a reason to stay.

My relationship fell apart in December. A few weeks later, I went away with two of my dear friends and I cried for Christmas. That is what I did. I walked on the beach and sat and cried. I listened to music and I cried. I opened little presents that reminded me of other presents I had given or received from my partner and I cried. I remembered we would never be old together or sleep in the same bed together or tell each other our dreams or decorate a room or talk in the wee hours of the morning. I cried. I remembered all the places we traveled and I wrote them down and remembered images of each place: a temple in Lhasa, a field in the Himalayas, Theresienstadt on the fiftieth anniversary of the Holocaust. Summers in pure blue water and walking, we were always walking. And meals and hummus and tomatoes and warm baths.

I cried for months, wailed at times, whimpered at others. And then I stopped crying. I began to breathe and find myself and slowly I began to get free. Grieving became freedom. Grieving led me organically and naturally to the next place.

There is a power that comes out of surrendering to grief and a power that is the result of refusing it. I think they are two very different types of power. The one that emerges through allowing grief feels clean, purged, and inclusive. You have experienced pain and grief so you would not want to inflict it on someone else. The kind of power that emerges through the denial of grief or the resistance to grief is aggressive power. It is trying to conquer something, annihilate something, and over-come something. It emerges out of fear and a need to protect oneself from a feeling, which then becomes a country, a people, et cetera. It is inauthentic power. It is not shamanic; one has not passed through something in order to arrive there. It is manufactured power in order to manipulate, bully, or deny. Because the central energy of this power is rooted in control or maintaining the illusion of control. This power is based on pushing something away. The power is based on the belief that there are victims and perpetrators. Usually the person wielding the power believes he is the victim and that some person or many people are out to get him. To grieve would mean letting go of this position, letting go of the need for position, the need for strategy or de-fense, being lost in the wave of grief. It would mean surrender.

THE WAVE THAT CAME AND
TOOK EVERYTHING AWAY

I n the middle of this grieving, a bigger wave came.
Its impact occupied the world. The tsunami of 2004
occurred about three weeks after my relationship
fell apart. There was something about a one-hundred-
foot wave rising up at 150 miles an hour within
minutes and destroying a totally unsuspecting world—
something about the utter unpredictability and the
loss—I knew I had to go to Sri Lanka.

After a few days there, I wrote this:

Today was easier.

*Maybe it was getting up at 4 A.M. in the dark hotel room in
Colombo, Sri Lanka, and drinking black coffee and chanting as
the sun began to rise over the Indian Ocean. Maybe it was the
hours of driving on the post-tsunami roads—the nuclear remains: uprooted mango trees, their stumps exposed like raw
cavities, the smashed and shattered concrete slabs that were
foundations, the muddied teddy bear flat on its back or the sin-*

gle turquoise plastic chair in the middle of what was once a patio. Maybe it was the randomness of what remains. The way objects arrange themselves in what might have been a life or many people's lives. The Sunday papers and a huge black boot and a toilet seat. They found 500 dead bodies in the village but only 190 of them were actually from there. The rest floated in from other places. Maybe it was the sea of swollen corpses or the children whose arms were still outstretched trying to stay connected. Or the sun-drenched Asian face of the ten-year-old girl in her school uniform as she grimaced after each name on the list of the people she had lost: my mother, my father, my sister, my brother. Little sad frowns that flashed like a nervous tic and would now be part of her character. Maybe it was the fisherman who couldn't blame the sea even though it took everything he had because it had once given him everything. Or the smell of the numbness of people who woke up Sunday morning without warning and started running from a forty-foot wall of water coming as fast as a racing airplane. Maybe it was the way they collected and cleaned and organized the remains of their china, stacking the little cups on one of the few remaining shelves in a house they could no longer sleep in as the walls might collapse. Or the way the villagers would now run whenever the sea got rough because they no longer could trust her intentions.

It was easier being without you. It was easier not pretending there was safety or anything certain or a place to come back to. How I wanted you to protect me. How I wanted to believe our love could prevent us from going under.

Do you know the only animals that died in the tsunami were the ones that were domesticated and caged? No wild animals drowned.

What drew me to Sri Lanka was the question of grief. How do people grieve? How do they process such loss and complete destruction? I needed to know the ways of grieving. I was drawn there to feel and see and touch the Indian Ocean—home of the wave that buried houses and memories, thousands of lives and livelihoods, within minutes. I needed to stand on those devastated beaches and see firsthand the uprooted mango trees, ancient headstones split apart, buses hanging from rooftops. I needed to know how the human brain and heart and spirit could process something so mythic and abrupt and random, how people go on in the face of such catastrophe.

The post-tsunami grief was a different kind of grief than I had experienced from war or violent losses. It wasn't the result of cruelty or hatred or revenge. The wave didn't focus on specific ethnic groups or religions or tribes. It wasn't personal. It didn't target specific neighborhoods or buildings or military installations. It didn't try to take out the leaders or artists or intellectuals. It happened without warning within minutes to everyone and everything in its path. It was brought on not by the rise of right-wing factions, or thugs, or stories about weapons of mass destruction.

It was triggered by the earth quaking. There were

no leaders or governments or armies to blame, only nature, only unseen forces, only God. And so the bitterness and betrayal and sense of victimization that I have
seen in war zones were simply not present. Many of
the people I spoke with had lived for generations by the
sea. They made their livings from the sea. And so
the sea was a major character in their story. That character had suddenly behaved in a shocking, surprising
way. Very few were prepared for it. Very few had yet
been able to make peace with it. I met hardly anyone, for example, who was fishing, eating fish, or even
going close to the water. Others were in hospitals, fighting infection, still choking on the sea. Some were still
afraid of going under. Some were just beginning to come
up for air.

But there was no one who felt singled out, felt the
sea had hurt them because of something they had done
or believed. There was loss: naked, massive, untenable
loss. The grief from the tsunami was as vast and deep
and organic as the Indian Ocean itself. Maybe it was because it wasn't corrupted by cruelty or torture. Maybe
it was simply the nature of water.

I spent days driving nearly a thousand kilometers
across the stunning landscape of Sri Lanka. I traveled
through Matara, Galle, Amparra, Kalmunai, Komari,
Battilacoa, and Pottuvil. I spoke with women in refugee
camps, storage rooms, temples, schools, churches, and
tents. There were moms who were numb and blank

and teenage girls who still had that raging spark. There were women compulsively sweeping and cleaning and women who didn't know where to start. There were young girls unable to close their eyes and older women who couldn't stop sleeping.

In every refugee site I visited, people literally lined up, as if waiting for food, to tell me their stories. All that mattered is that I had time to listen. As one person spoke, many in the community gathered around to hear. Everyone was at different stages of grieving, feeling, believing. The telling of the story, particularly to an outsider, was a crucial ritual. Even those who were still numb from the agony of loss needed to talk. Each story had a kind of process, a journey of melting and grieving.

When we began the interview, Padminie did not look at me. She stared out as if focused on another time and place. Her name means "lotus," the only flower that blossoms and seeds at the same time. When the tsunami came, she was in the fishing village of Moraketiara, off Dickwella. She was cooking rice and coconut for breakfast for her husband and two children—one daughter who was fifteen, one son who was twelve. The waves were coming very fast, very unusual. The family got frightened. "This is very unlike other days," the husband said. "We will run away." He grabbed the son.

Padminie grabbed the daughter. By the time they got out of the house the water was up to their waist. Behind the house was a fence. They tried to climb up it, but it collapsed. The husband held on to her blouse. They were all connected. Padminie said, "We will all die together." Then her husband lost his grip on her blouse. The two pairs separated. She with their daughter. He with their son. The daughter was crying, "What's going to happen to us?" Then the second wave came. Padminie was pulled under the water and lost the child. The water was so forceful it stripped off her clothes. It took her a long distance.

After a while, she suddenly felt stationary. She was stopped somehow, caught. It turned out her long, long black hair had wrapped around a barbed-wire fence and was holding her there.

At first she thought she had lost her entire family. Then she found her husband. He had seen her and the daughter passing by in the water. The son clung to his father's hair, but the water uprooted a tree and carried the son away. Later they found the child alive, but he died soon after from sand in his lungs. "I never found my daughter. We searched for three days. About fifteen bodies had washed up in the lagoon. We searched through them and the debris."

When she described this searching through the dead bodies, Padminie began to cry. It was the first time she was really there with me. She was feeling her children missing. Telling the story seemed to concretize the catastrophe. The wind was blowing and there were waves moving behind her in the lagoon. Padminie was momentarily alive. She asked me to wait. She went off and then quickly returned with two rescued water-damaged photographs of her daughter and son. It was crucial that I see them. It was crucial that I acknowledge their beauty and their existence. This telling and this showing of pictures, even though fraught with the deepest sorrow, were her tiny steps toward beginning.

For many people in Sri Lanka, finding the body or the remains of the loved one's body was a crucial part of separation and grieving. Because of the fear of disease, many people did not have a chance to identify their loved ones before the bodies were buried or burned. Others were luckier and were able to touch and acknowledge their dead. This concrete act made loss tangible, made death definite.

Melani was madly in love with her husband. They had four children together. When she realized her husband had been washed away with one of her children, she wanted to commit suicide. People grabbed her and took her to the hospital. She was bleeding. She didn't notice, as she was so obsessed with finding her husband. First she searched through the dead bodies at the hospital. Then she went to the injured bodies. She saw

a dead body on a trolley already stiff. She knew it was
he. There wasn't enough room in the mortuary. She
wanted to take him out. She went through a complicated process until she finally got the body. Then she
realized she had no money and no place to take it. In
the end, she decided to leave her husband in the hospital. But finding his body allowed her to make a connection with him, allowed her to begin her mourning.

For many survivors, visiting the place where their
houses once stood was a crucial part of grieving. It was
the remembering and the cherishing of their former existence that allowed them to begin to release it.

Buddhicka was sixteen. Her name means "wise
girl." She had been cleaning when the wave came suddenly. She watched her grandmother be electrocuted
when her house exploded from the impact of the wave.
She lost her brother and sister and her aunts. A six-inch
rusty nail punctured her stomach. She was in the hospital for nine days believing everyone in her family was
gone. On the tenth day, she found her mother in the
same ward. She told me, "I go to my house, or where
my house used to be, every day. I have to do this re-
peatedly. I do this to remember what happened." I
asked her to take me there.

It was hot, blue skies and a sultry wind. The sea was
inviting and innocent. The beach looked postnuclear.

There were smoky places that seemed like summer bonfires, but it turned out they were burning piles of decomposed corpses. New ones washed up every day and disintegrated when they were lifted. There were incidental funeral pyres along the way, bones and the skull of a ten-year-old boy that looked like the shell of a coconut. The beach was a graveyard. We reached Buddhicka's house and all that was left was a red cement foundation. She showed me where her bedroom had been. "My room had the best view of the sea," she told me. It was clearly staggering. All her family had lived in a row of houses. She showed me how she could go out the back door directly to her aunts' house. She told me, "My aunts would come over every night to watch television. I would give up everything material if I could get them back." We stood in what was once her bedroom, and I watched Buddhicka's young face as her brain did everything it could to make sense of what had happened. She was caught between the present and the past. I saw how necessary it was for her to be in the actual place where she had once lived. It was her foundation. A red concrete childhood that would, if honored and remembered, give birth to her future.

How do people go on when just about everything they own and love is gone? They wash their borrowed clothes and hang them out to dry. They cook familiar food rations, rice and dahl, and eat them together, in a circle.

They dream that their drowned mothers are smiling at them. They dress their daughters in the donated white Sunday dharma dresses so their daughters can feel pretty and spiritual even though they are sleeping on the floor of the temple. They grieve by participating in the ordinary.

I sat with a mother, Osante, and her daughter-in-law, Polhane, in a house where the floors were cracked in half. The clock had stopped at 9:15, when it had been submerged in the wave. They could no longer live in this house, but they had cleaned and stacked the few teacups they had gathered from the water and ground on the one remaining shelf. These cups were the story of the future. These cups were their little memories and possibilities. Osante said, "We picked the china off the floor. It was floating around. We needed to save something."

Dolci lost her older brother, who drowned in the train with almost three thousand others. Her brother had always taken care of her when she was a child. The only survivor of his family was his ten-year-old daughter, Utera, who miraculously was lifted to the top of the train and then rescued by strangers. Dolci was totally crushed by the loss of her brother, but she found her purpose. She said, "I loved my elderly brother. I want to repay him by educating his daughter. That will make his life matter."

I asked Buddhicka what she needed and wanted the most. She said, "I want other young people to know that there are refugee camps like this all over the world. They should go and help. It doesn't have to be a tsunami." She tells me, "All I want now is to go to school. That is the only thing that gives me hope. I want to do art." When she talks about school her whole being lights up and you can tell who she was once, just a month ago, before the waves came to her village, Kalmunai.

I asked Farsana, who was seven months pregnant, how she was dealing with the loss of her home. How does she go on? She said, "I believe it's the work of God." She was very firm when she said, "I don't want to live elsewhere. I still like the ocean. If it happens again in the future, it will be the will of God. I will relate the story to my child." I asked her if she has been back to the water. She laughed and said, "None of us feel safe going there." I asked her if she'd go with me. She took this as a challenge and agreed.

The sun was out, blue sky and green-blue water. We walked through what used to be a beautiful gathering of houses on the beach. There was nothing now but broken branches and debris. Slowly and carefully we walked to the water's edge. Farsana was dressed in

flowing yellow and purple salwar kameez. I supported
her as she rolled up her pants and we walked into the
sea. The water was warm and soft and caressing. She
was hugely pregnant. The waves were gentle now, but
they could get stronger. They could become anything.
We held hands in the water. Farsana slowly let herself
breathe. And then she started giggling and giggling.

Padminie tells her story and begins to cry. Buddhicka
sits in the memory of her bedroom and imagines school.
Dolci raises her dead brother's daughter, Utera. Pregnant Farsana finds her way back into the water. These
are the ways women remain fluid like water. These are
the ways of grieving.

LEAVING MY FATHER'S HOUSE

I am leaving my father's house
Stepping out
Stepping off
Free falling outside the confines
Of what is acceptable or known.
I am leaving this cage
Which suppressed
Depressed
Made less of me
So thoroughly
I came to call it my legacy
My country
My home.
I am leaving those angry men
Whose broken hearts and wounds
Became more painful and urgent
Than my own.
I am not going to be sorry anymore

Or responsible or wrong.
I am not going to give everything
That is mine
And call it yours.
I am going to stop believing
I can wake you up
Or break open your shell
Or get you to feel
Your sorrow your grief
Your tenderness
I am going to stop mainlining my life force
Into your self-esteem:
Air pump girl blowing up boy rubber ball
You can stay flat and go nowhere by yourself.
I am leaving my father's house
I am not going to whisper anymore or tiptoe
Or lie flat on my back,
I am not ducking, flinching, waiting till you finish
Or whimpering in the dark.
I am moving out.
I am not going back.
I am leaving my father's house
'Cause
I no longer believe your lies
About freedom and democracy
That it hurts you more
Than your whips or words or policies hurt me.
I am going to believe what I see:

Bruises on my neck
Floating corpses in the streets
Iraqi women with their voting fingers
Chopped off
Emaciated polar bears
Melting from corporate greed.
I am leaving your guilt-tripping fear-inducing
Evil-projecting idea of me.
I am fleeing your disguised terror of my bigness,
My hunger, my vagina, my compassion,
My tongue.
I am leaving my father's house
I see how it is punishing spinning
Out insanely in paranoid desperation
Dividing the world into
Evildoers and saints.
I am leaving my father's house
I do not want a position there
I will not imitate your cold tactics
To get a seat on the floor
I will not leash your prisoners
Or jerk them off
I will not starve your workers
Organize lynch mobs
Or camouflage your crimes
I will not be tits and ass on your arm
Or smile till my face breaks off.
I am leaving my father's house

Corporate towers
Cathedrals, mosques, and synagogues
Picket-fenced houses and Pentagons.
I am going out
Past
The neighborhoods
Nations
Fundamental doctrines
And misinterpreted laws.
Past the reach of your fist
Past the fire breath of your rage
Past the tentacles of your seductive melancholy
Or your unspoken promises to change.
I am willing to be alone, disliked, slandered
And misconstrued
Because my freedom is more important
Than your so-called love.
Because my leaping
Will be the ultimate jumping off
Will be the new beginning
Without a daddy in charge,
On top
In control
Of all the goods, ideas,
Interpretations, and cash.
I am going out there by myself
But I know I will find the rest of you there

Waiting
Ready
Knee-deep in the garden
Hands raised in the water
Way way out past my father's house.

IV

FINALLY EXPOSED—
INSECURE AT LAST

SMACK IN THE CENTER OF AMERICA

In the fall of 2005 I was on a six-month North American tour with my play *The Good Body*. It was grueling and profound: the intense marathon of performing eight shows a week; the constant moving; the new hotel room every few days; new, almost soft sheets; new, not right pillows; new path to the toilet to negotiate in the middle of the night; new size and feel of the audience—sometimes full and unresponsive, sometimes scraggly and wild—new stage; new crew; new follow-spot operators each with a particular way of shining or not shining the light on me. And, of course, there was the play itself, which threw me night after night into the center of my self-hatred, my sense of never being enough, my longing for a mother, the betrayal of my father. The constant reminder that I was now alone in this world at fifty-two, standing on a stage by myself, telling my truth in front of strangers.

I was there smack in the center of the loneliness and

longing of America, smack in the center of the good-
ness of those who are seeking a way out of this paradigm. I was there as the alchemy of the play worked its
daily magic on me, like a laboratory, slowly metaboliz-
ing and transforming my remaining attachment to notions of security. I stopped reading reviews (well, most
of the time); I stopped looking for confirmation, for
identity. I began to cherish the most quiet, vocally unresponsive crowd because it forced me to go in further,
into myself, to be more true, to not rely on the currents
of approval or applause. So I could become more of
who I am and trust that the play would reach whoever
it was meant to reach. I learned to stop moving fast. I
learned to breathe. To find my way to the next beat
without prop or charm or playing for laughs. To sit in
the uncertainty, to find my way in front of the audience
as it was happening, to let my insecurities be apparent.

The play became my teacher, invited me to live in
the vast wilderness of question and emptiness, to fall
into the despair of aloneness and the exultation when
something true suddenly arrived in my body.

I was there each night smack in the middle of
America, smack in the middle of the empire as it was
falling, crumbling. As the years of this particular administration added up and the consequences of a fascist
storm revealed themselves. The American levee was
broken. The polluted waters were moving in; the wave
broke down the shoreline, the bodies of the dead float-

ing facedown in Iraq and New Orleans. The hidden prisons of torture were found and revealed, along with the illegal leaks and blatant lies that justified a war that had now killed thousands of people. The arctic ice caps melting, the hurricanes and earthquakes, the nearly starved polar bears, the racist tides carrying the once shackled slaves who were now drowned in poverty and neglect, the instruments of torture washed up in the storm, the hoods and the echoes of ugly words and electrical prongs.

In March 2006, I interviewed Malalai Joya, who was elected to the 249-seat National Assembly, Wolesi Jirga, in September 2005 as a representative of Farah Province in Afghanistan. After she spoke out publicly in 2003 before the grand council, known as the Loya Jirga, against the domination of warlords, her life was threatened by four assassination attempts and she was forced to wear a burqa and be accompanied by four bodyguards as she traveled throughout Afghanistan. She asked me, "If there is democracy and freedom in our country, why do I receive death threats day after day, why do they attack my office, not allow me to speak in Parliament?" Except for Kabul, where there were some women who had jobs, where it was not mandatory to wear burqas, where there were a handful of women ministers and members of Parliament, she told me the situation for women throughout the rest of the country had not fundamentally changed.

"The U.S. replaced the Taliban with the Northern Alliance. These warlords learned the talk of democracy, they wear the suits and ties, but it is still the Taliban mentality. Women are raped, their children are kidnapped, they are not permitted to go to school, they kill themselves."

My friend Sarah Chayes, a reporter for NPR, wrote me in the winter of 2006 from Kandahar, Afghanistan, where she moved a few years ago. She said that the U.S. was so busy going after imaginary al-Qaeda members and suicide bombers supposedly in Afghanistan that they had failed to protect the Afghan people from the rise of the Taliban, who were murdering and intimidating in her part of the country. She said that many of the people of Kandahar now believed the United States was in cahoots with the Taliban. Meanwhile, we had allowed al-Qaeda to secure serious ground in Iraq, the place we had been supposedly liberating. The U.S. was pursuing ghosts everywhere in the name of security: imaginary weapons in Iraq, suicide bombers in Kandahar, misreported bombs on the New York City subways. Millions of dollars were being spent on these false alarms while the real security of people was undermined everywhere in the world. This aggressive and illegal pursuit itself had actually undermined security. The images of tortured Arabs in illegal prisons and holding places like Guantánamo, the smoldering bodies of dead Taliban members burned by U.S. soldiers, the desecrated Koran. The televised bombing and melting of thousands of innocent Iraqi children in Al-Falluja. Guernica-like atrocities such as these had created more potential terrorists, more raging Islamic youths.

The people who were supposedly protecting us gave license to immoral and atrocious practices like illegal wiretapping and holding prisoners without charges or rights, removing our voice and rights, creating tyranny. And people permitted this, remaining blind to everything in their desperation for protection and security.

Each night that I stood onstage, I stood in the center of this storm. I stood in the center of a country that had been sold a lie about security and had, since September 11, allowed our government to destroy our environment, our democracy, our education, our health care, our morality, our standing in the world, our freedom, and our idea of ourselves for this illusion. I stood on a platform and felt how deeply distracted Americans were by their corporate-rigged self-hatred, by their sense that they were not enough, that they did not know enough, that they had to surrender their will and imagination and instincts and morality to the rich and Ivy Leagued and powerful who convinced them through corporate takeover and fear and mind control that they need to consume product after product to make themselves thinner, prettier, lighter, tighter—that somehow this consumption would ultimately lead to their security. I stood on the stage and I felt in my bones the loneliness and pointlessness of this pursuit. I felt the isolation that this pursuit has engendered. I felt the exploitation of the world's peoples and resources through this ravenous pursuit. I felt the unexpressed guilt in the people who knew they were being manipulated and still they could not stop consuming. I felt the depth of insecurity it has created, and the sorrow. I felt the wide-open empty space of America—not just in the physical geography of the country but in our psyche.

The world has the wrong ideas about Americans. Americans are deeply kind, good, and thoughtful people. It is not aggression or hatred. Americans are generous and open.

It is not even apathy or lack of caring. It is a paralysis that comes from malignant self-hatred. It is the frozenness that comes from a suffocating loneliness. It is a story in the center of the culture that there are those who are beautiful and smart and rich. They are good, and the rest of us are pathetic, lost, worthless, and not enough. Each night I stood in the center of this. Each night after the show audience members stopped me on the street. They told me how fat they felt or ugly or stupid or how they just couldn't figure it out. Each night they told me how they were starving themselves or stuffing themselves or hiding or taking drugs.

I wanted to throw myself on the stage as in a Greek drama and wail and wail and pull my hair and scream: This is not accidental what you feel. This is not per-

sonal. There is a plan to make you feel ugly and powerless, insignificant and insecure. There is a plan to make
you feel like someone or something is coming to fix and
rescue you. Give up illusions of security! There is no
one coming to take death or aging or sickness away.
There is no solution. There is no reason to fix it. No one
smarter or better or on top. You are already enough.
Enough. Each and every one of you. Enough. Enough.

DOWN TO THE ZERO OF MYSELF

Here on the road, I am nothing, an erased being, down to the zero of myself. Lonely. They forgot me again, left me, alone. Forever by myself. Abandoned. The clinking martini glasses in the distance, the beautiful and laughing who own this world. I did not want to come here—to this place on the road. I did not want to return to the depths of emptiness in myself, to this place of being lost, of never being remembered, of never existing. My father reduced me with his hands, his fists, his belts, his words. Then afterward, in that terrible room of emptiness and shame, I got down and pressed myself against the green scratchy wall-to-wall carpet, rocked myself over and over, "someone someone someone."

I return to that room in myself, that emptiness, that terrible place that never went away. I pressed myself against naked sweaty teenage boys in wet night grass so it would go away. I allowed your grown-up man hands all over my girl flesh so it would go away. I smoked Camels and marijuana and drank bottles of gin and took off my clothes and did methedrine. Anything to make it go away. I became driven and mad with work and was charming and rousing and inspirational and devoted and committed and willing to risk everything. I slept with married mad men and sad men and pretty mean blond women.

Now I swim in the center of it. No crowds, no audiences, no accolades, no accomplishments, nothing soothes it or keeps it at bay.

Nothing. Finally down to the zero of myself. Fully insecure. On the road. In the center of nowhere. In the anxiety mall.

DIVING

When I was a child I loved diving. Diving off. Diving in. Diving off high stone quarry walls. Diving off high diving boards. I loved climbing the long ladder to the top. I loved my sky blue one-piece bathing suit. I loved how fast and compact I was at ten. I loved practicing the approach. I see now everything is in the approach. How high you get, how focused your attention, how clear your desire for flight and clean entry. I loved my naked wet feet on the board. Loved the three steps, knee up, jump down on the bounce. I loved flying through time and space. Loved altering my body in air, loved moving with currents, loved grace. Loved flipping sometimes, or opening up like a swan. Loved entering the water without a trace (this happened very rarely). Loved the force of the dive pushing me deeper, pushing me under. Loved getting out of the water and doing it all over again. Loved practicing. Loved coming out of the pool with

my hair slicked back, it made me feel like a water animal. Loved the way the water dripped and fell out of
my bathing suit when I walked back to the board.
Loved wearing a sweatshirt when I practiced 'cause it
made me feel brave. Loved my diving instructor. He
was handsome and angular. His name was Jake.

Then there was my father and it all changed. He
would sit in a deck chair by the pool.

He called it "observing me"—like I was a storm
brewing or some bacteria in a petri dish or something
about to go bad. It made me nervous, him sitting there,
smoking Lucky Strikes and observing me. It changed
the nature of what I was doing. It made me aware of
myself. It made me afraid. It made me think about what
he was thinking rather than just flying through space.
After each dive I would surface from the pool and he
would give me a thumbs-up or a thumbs-down. Mostly
it was thumbs-down. He was so serious. I couldn't mess
up. But I did, over and over. I began to dive for his love,
for his approval. Not for the joy of the jump on the
bounce, or flying through space or making my body do
new things. I began to sell my dives, began to see them
as hard currency. Things that could win my father's af-
fection. It is where I learned to perform. High-diving
girl-hooker tricks.

Sometimes I would look at him and try to guess
what he was thinking during the dive and I would end
up smashing my chest into the water. Sometimes I was

so sure he hated what I was doing that I would ruin the dive before he could criticize me. On the rare occasion I got a thumbs-up, I would usually quit for the day 'cause I was so so scared of failing after that. I lost the pleasure. I lost the privacy. I lost the discovery. I lost what was mine.

I had to be someone. My dives had to be the greatest. I had to be better than anyone else. I wasn't diving anymore. I was racing, I was proving myself, I was trying to win.

This became the trajectory of my life. Racing, not diving. Winning, not discovering, Proving, not learning. Conquering, not being.

I think how much I have read that I did not read. I think how little I was able to learn. Information became currency. Know what you need to maintain security. Memorize facts in order to pass the exams. I think how many places I have traveled that I did not see, how many times I have had sex without losing myself 'cause I was so worried about performing. I think how my father has been sitting there as I come up from a dive—a new piece I have written or a speech I have given. I think how many years I have longed for the weight of his gaze to be lifted and how at the same time I was afraid to lose it since I believed it was what motivated me and gave me direction.

I think how I learned then to compare myself to others and compete. How anyone who won at anything was the proof of what a loser I was. How desperate I was to win and how much shame I felt around my own desperation. Losing became so unbearable that eventually I turned to alcohol and drugs so I could stop engaging or competing at all. But even as a drunk, I had to be the worst, had to be the craziest, had to push myself to the edge. That way I would be the most significant loser. I think how, in the mad struggle to get where I thought I needed to go, I had no time or ability to ever be anywhere that I was.

And now I was about to open *The Good Body* in Washington, D.C., heart of the empire where government and corporations merge in greed and exploitation, turning the majority of the world into losers. Stupid me, to have thought I had something to say in the face of this power and arrogance and privilege. There I was, in another empty hotel room, e-mails coming in every minute from women all over the world with news of continuing violations—from Yanar in Iraq in the darkest time of her country, unable to leave her house for fear of being gunned down by religious extremists the U.S. had unleashed in this ungodly war; from Esther, whose center, Casa Amiga, was desperate for funds as the bodies of poor factory women continued to turn up dead in Ciudad Juárez. I was alone, without a partner, feeling fat and old, comparing myself to everything and everyone shiny and successful and significant. I was back on the diving board, rushing my dive, not concentrating, not focused on what I love, looking out another millionth time for his—for the world's—thumbs-up. I was missing my step on the board, landing flat on my chest, smashing and hurting myself, no grace. Flopping. Never amounting to anything. Never, never being anyone.

I stopped fighting it. I dissolved. I became no one. I lay on the floor and I cried and cried. I passed through to the other side. Then I passed out. I slept like I have never slept. I slept as if I had died.

The next day, my eyes swollen, I went for a walk in the capital. I was so tired and fragile. But there was this lightness, this sweetness, in me. I remembered it from long ago.

Out of nowhere I heard this gentle voice say, very matter-of-factly, "You are done. You already did it. You made something of your life. You can stop. You already dove for him. You can live your life now. Go on."

I breathed. It was hard to believe.

That night I opened in Washington, D.C. It was different this time. I was not thinking about how it looked or how I was being received. I was not thinking about critics or other playwrights or what I was going to be doing next to prove my worth. I was deeply in the story, flying through space, through currents of thoughts and feelings. I was lost in the mystery. I was dancing in the messy, wet world of the play. There were hundreds of people in the audience, yet no one was watching. I was not separated from them by my need for their approval. We were there together, struggling to find our way, working on our approach, our bounce, our courage, our height, our spin, our grace, our entry.

My father was no longer in his chair smoking and observing. He was gone. He got the first fifty-two years of my life. The next ones are for diving.

CHRISTMAS EVE, 2005

was alone. The phone did not ring. There was no e-mail. There was not even snow. The city had emptied. There was no family gathered around my tree. I cooked for myself: a veggie burger, some vegetarian chili, some corn. I ate it and I took my time. I loved my new plates. I loved the candles and the Christmas flowers. I loved how cozy my aloneness had become. There was no drug I wanted to take to escape this emptiness. I had been sober twenty-eight years.

There were desires—to learn Arabic, to be more accurate, to be with my mother without bitterness, complaint, or aversion when she died, to stop comparing myself to anyone, to end violence and poverty, to get lost in India—some simple things.

It had not turned out the way I expected, most of this. I did not kill myself in my twenties. I did not remain poor. I found my way back to my family. I could sometimes even appreciate that it was my father who was the person who had taught me not to lie. I was no longer depressed. I was still equally attracted to men and women. I was not sure that I believed or had ever believed in monogamous live-in relationships. I did not have illusions that anything I was feeling would last.

There was nothing I wanted. There was no place I was going. There was no one I longed to meet who might change all this.

IN THE NAME OF SECURITY, THEY SOMEHOW FORGOT TO PROTECT THE PEOPLE

Hurricane Katrina was the greatest natural disaster in American history, and our money, our will, our energy, were spent thousands of miles away—supposedly defending our security. What happened in New Orleans—what is still happening in New Orleans—is an undeniable and devastating example of how the little security we can expect and are rightfully entitled to gets consistently undermined and jeopardized by the hope of this false and impossible übersecurity. As Sophie, a woman caught in the nightmare of the New Orleans convention center, said to me, "You're paying for a war over there when you should be helping people here."

I went to New Orleans nearly nine months after Katrina. It was there that I saw how in the pursuit of security the government forgot to protect the people.

This, of course, has been happening for decades, but the criminal abandonment, the saturating trauma, the paralysis, the depression, and the humiliation in the drowned delta bowl have made it undeniable.

Everything in post-Katrina New Orleans can be measured in terms of the presence or absence of the brown water line that stains the houses and stores and churches like markings of the plague. The line indicates how deeply infected, how destroyed the building is, how much potential loss and death and destruction have been visited there. The higher the line on the building, the worse the outcome. In some parts of town there is no line on the houses, indicating wealth and privilege, or luck and salvation—or the opposite: total engulfment in water.

Then there are the strange spray-painted markings on the houses: the date, usually accompanied by some determination—*possible body, dog taken, TFC* (totally free of content). A circle with a line through it is the most ominous, indicating a found dead body. I wonder over and over why these searches to find people in their houses didn't occur before the storm, before the water, when there was still time to save lives.

In many of the wards, particularly the Lower Ninth and Saint Bernard Parish, the story of Katrina gets told through the surreal arrangement of remaining objects. Houses sitting on cars or Laundromats. Piles of belongings randomly arranged or collected: a trophy and a condom, a hula hoop and a tie. The first day I was there, I came upon a white van filled with women driving around looking for puppies because stray hungry bitches were giving birth. They were no longer collecting cats, as the cats had all gone feral by then.

And there was the strange collection of signs:

GUTTING

WE TEAR DOWN HOUSES

1-800-AID-MOLD

So much was turned on its head. The old Lord & Taylor was the new—well, shall we say, the designated— Charity Hospital. MASH tents in the lobby could accommodate only twenty emergency patients. Frozen escalators were just memories of better shopping days. A dressing room in the evening-wear department, where southern daughters once modeled fancy cotillion gowns for their mothers, was now the barren sexual-assault clinic where women were being examined in stirrups for rapists' sperm.

Folks who live in New Orleans have always lived in the wet heart of insecurity. As one woman said to me, "We love it here because it is fertile and vulnerable." There is a six-month period every year called hurricane season. People prepare for and expect disaster. There is something about living on this edge, living in the direct and open path of the storm, that has made folks in New Orleans open, party-friendly, and deeply attached to community. They live waiting for the other shoe to drop. I interviewed a FEMA PR representative who had lived in New Orleans his whole life. I assumed it was his Marine Corps background that had driven him to create the "half-tank rule" for his family (must have a half tank of gas in the car at all times in case you need to escape) and to insist that each of his brothers and sisters carry a safety pack. I assumed he was an anomaly until I mentioned his tactics to two local women at dinner, both of whom immediately said they too followed the half-tank rule and, although they had a less thorough safety pack, they carried one just the same. They were impressed with the marine's kit, which included a throwaway phone, a one-hundred-dollar gas card, water-purifying tabs, wet wipes (which become your bathtub), granola bars, a change of clothes, tools to build a solar water heater, a flashlight, a weather radio, batteries, Off!, insurance information (optional), and a disposable camera. The women actually took notes so they could be more prepared in the future.

Most of the people I interviewed had lived through

Betsy and Camille. One woman told me she loved New Orleans. "That's why I came back for more punishment. And that's what I am getting."

It was not the storm that undid the people of New Orleans. It was not the levees breaking, although the destruction that the flooding wrought was massive and mind-blowing. What undid the folks of New Orleans was, and remains, the lack of response, the feeling of being forgotten, the absence of a plan, the waiting, the humiliations that occurred on the backs of humiliations. The disrespect.

In almost every story I heard, people were able to survive the natural disaster and even the man-influenced catastrophe of the levees breaking. It was what came afterward that broke them. One woman said, "There were three disasters. The first was the storm, the second was the levees breaking, the third was FEMA."

Sandrah, a sixty-six-year-old African American grandmother, had escaped the storm, managed to avoid getting caught in the water, and lived through the nightmare of the Superdome: the shock and terror of suddenly having to leave her house, the hours of waiting outside in line in the rain with thousands, the one wet blanket to sleep on amid the panicked masses in a stadium with a leaking roof, the lack of food and water, the not urinating for hours for fear of being raped in the bathroom. She survived all this and stayed strong for the two of her ten children who were with her.

Then there were the promised buses. She waited for five days. When they finally arrived, thousands lined up, jammed and panicked like caged animals. After hours, Sandrah and her children managed to make it to a bus.

"There, at the door, was a white soldier, a National Guard, with a pointed machine gun. He was telling us to take two steps back. Of course this was impossible 'cause we were wall-to-wall people. It was impossible to step back. You couldn't do it. But you had to or he wouldn't let you on the bus. It was a kind of tease. There were older people and people in wheelchairs. He made them all take two steps back. It was there that my faith failed me. My faith failed me at the bus door. The guard was in his fifties. He was cruel, a torturer. He was standing there with his gun. The sky was getting cloudy again. You didn't know if you were getting on the bus. Whether you would get out alive. Can you imagine someone teasing you with your life?"

Sandrah's faith failed momentarily, but it has since come back. "God cared about me. I made it through. A lot of people got sick after and just died." Sandrah's daughter Kenya was not so lucky. As I sat on the plastic-wrapped sofa interviewing the family, Kenya seemed unable to move or function. She had become seriously depressed while staying in a shelter after losing everything she had made and owned. She felt like a failure because she could not be strong like her mother. She ended up drinking half a bottle of cleaning fluid. She was very pregnant now and I couldn't help wondering if she drank it early on in her pregnancy, knowing she was carrying a new life, knowing she had no home, no job, no future.

After only a few days in New Orleans I, too, felt tired and heavy. The toxic particles from the air and ground and shame coated my throat. Like most of the folks in New Orleans, I was having a hard time sleeping or getting up, remembering, or finding reasons to be alive.

It wasn't the insecurity that did people in. It was the lack of care, in many cases the downright cruelty. This trauma was different from the trauma I experienced in the survivors of Sri Lanka after the tsunami. There, no one felt blamed for living by the water, no one was turned away from help at gunpoint, no one was called a refugee inside her own country.

I witnessed in the people of New Orleans a deep, agonizing sense that no help was coming, that they had been forgotten. In fact, many people I interviewed had come to believe that this was planned long ago to consciously get rid of them. A seventy-four-year-old African American man stayed at home after the levees broke, " 'cause I didn't want to get caught up in the nonsense at the Superdome. But I stayed home too long. When I walked out of my house in the pitch black of night, the water was up to my neck. I could only see the moon above. It was the scariest moment of my life."

He testified that he heard the levees blow. "I heard a boom." He believed they used dynamite. He believed that the corporations who run Las Vegas casinos had always wanted this land in order to build a new Las Vegas. He believed they flooded the wards to drive the people from their places so they could steal it out from under them.

He was not the only one who thought this. In the African American community this belief runs deep. And why wouldn't it? Most of those who once lived in New Orleans are still evacuees in strange towns and cities where they have no houses and no jobs and no incentive or ability to return home. Those that have come back have returned to madness: landlords who have increased rents from three hundred to nine hundred or twelve hundred dollars a month, water bills and electric bills for water and electricity that don't exist. No schools, no medical coverage, no hospitals, no mental-health support for a severely traumatized population. No answers on the condition of the levees, no real reckoning or accountability about anything. No stores, no jobs, no insurance. Outside workers being hired instead of the locally unemployed to rebuild the houses. No safe doors on their tin FEMA trailers. A policeman said, "You could break into these trailers with a butter knife." No report on the toxicity of the neighborhoods or a cleanup plan for the future. No reliable political infrastructure. Ecoee, a severely overworked nurse in the sexual-assault unit at Lord & Taylor, told me, "We're all passengers in the van waiting for someone to drive it. We don't have keys or a driver's license."

I sat with Sophie on a porch, where she was periodically holding or minding someone else's baby. She was exhausted and furious. She was fifty and had just returned to the projects. Her story seems to epitomize everything.

"I lived in New Orleans all my life. I loved it here. Loved the people, loved where I live. I was raised here in the Guste Public Housing. All of us came up as a family. We stayed friends. I have four kids. One is deceased ten years. He was shot thirty-two times in New Orleans. We lost our children here. My child shed his blood. We own this place and have a right to it.

"We prepared for the storm. We got groceries. We assumed the storm would hit and be over. That is what usually happened.

"When the storm hit, the whole foundation of the projects shook. The windows blew out. The air conditioner twisted. Girl, you be about to get sucked out! Then the door slammed and took the tip off my fourteen-year-old boy's finger. I didn't know what to do. When

your child is hurt you tend to lose it. Blood gushing. I
called 911. They told me I should have left already.
I could not have fucking left! I had no transportation,
no ride. They told me they couldn't come. They asked
me to bring my child. They said it wasn't an emergency.
They told me to hold his finger. The blood was gushing
more. I fell to my knees and I prayed. I need to help my
child. I crushed ice and I wrapped it around his finger. I
felt it was all my fault. I gave my son a Tylenol. I lost a
child before. I was insane. All the time I kept shaking
him to make sure he wasn't dying. I put my head on his
chest. I would die if something happened to that child
in my house.

"Later, I asked people to bring me to the hospital.
There was martial law but this was a medical emergency. We didn't know the levees had broken. It was
bright and sunny. When I finally got to Charity Hospital a member of the National Guard cocked his gun on
me. I told him, 'You can kill me if you want, but my
child needs help.' He thought I was loony, but he let me
in. My child had been in the house from seven A.M. to
three P.M. with part of his finger missing. They rushed
him to the bed. They needed to do surgery. The doctors
made me feel comfortable. They reassured me. They
said they could sew his finger back on. They said it
would be shorter. My child kept telling me not to feel
guilty. He kept saying it wasn't my fault.

"When we went outside after the surgery it was

about eight-thirty P.M. There was a curfew. I was praying they wouldn't shoot me. I got home. They kept
telling us the water was coming. I thought they were
playing games with us. The radio was out of batteries.
People say things to make people panic. But the water
was really coming. It was coming in the streets. It was
coming full force. Nobody had told people to leave.
There were helicopters. Everyone started freaking out,
waving, watching the water come up. The water was
up to our chest. Garbage was coming out of the water.
It was filthy. I didn't want to go in it. Particularly with
my son who had just had surgery. I went upstairs in our
high-rise building. We sat up all night. I called my ex-
husband. He said, 'You need to come from out of there.'

"I decided to bring my child to the convention center. The water was up to our necks. It was awful and
stinky. It was doing things to people. They were putting babies in ice chests. There were wiggling things—
maggots, alligators, bodies—in the water. There was a
child refusing to go in it, screaming, 'There are mon-
sters in the water!' You had to be so careful where you
stepped. If you missed the curb or stepped in the hole
where a manhole cover had been blown away, you
could go under the water.

"We finally made it to a dry street. It was actually
called Dry Street. Or it used to be called Dry Street. People were looting the stores. Some were looking for

clothes to wear that weren't funky. Some were looking
to sell clothes.

"The convention center was terrible. No food. No
water. I did not have a change of clothes. I stunk. Lord
have mercy! The whole city of New Orleans was at the
convention center. I didn't know there were so many
people. It was hell there. Everyone was just crying.
Shootings were breaking out. Everyone running and
trampling. People dropping dead. I was in my dirty
clothes for days. Cold at night. Hot during the day.
Chaos. No one was in charge.

"At one point, we decided to stay outside the center.
Then someone said water was coming. Everyone panicked and started running. There was a stampede.
Knocked down the elderly. I thought my leg was broken. Military suddenly arrived in a truck. The National
Guard. I have no idea how many there were of them.
They jumped out and put rifles to our heads, 'Motherfuckers! Bitches!' they said. 'Lay down. Don't move,
motherfuckers.' We lay facedown flat down on the as-
phalt.

"I still have nightmares, all these months later."

Sophie's best friend, Patricia, was listening with us
on the porch. "Sophie, tell them about the Magic Markers." They both laughed a crazy laugh.

Sophie said, "At one point during the storm, the
mayor told everyone to get a permanent Magic Marker

and write their Social Security number on their inner forearm. I wasn't going to do that! That mayor wasn't going to tell me I was going to die. And besides, where would us poor people ever get a permanent Magic Marker?"

Looking at a diagram of all the places where the levees had breached, entitled "Multiple Failure," I couldn't help marveling at the irony. I was thinking about all the multiple failures involved in Katrina. I was thinking about the word "breach." Breach of promise. Breach of security. Breach of trust. I was thinking what "breach" means: to fail to obey, keep, or preserve something, for example, a law or commitment, a breakdown in friendly relations, a gap that results when something or somebody leaves.

I was thinking of how the experience before, during, and after Katrina in New Orleans was a massive political and spiritual breach. We failed to preserve the laws of human decency. I was thinking of the hole that was left when the local and national governments abandoned the wildly waving people.

We have all been wrongly manipulated, misguided to believe we are longing for security, when really it is kindness we are after. There would be no reason to

build fences or walls or lock our doors, no reason to drop
scud missiles, no reason to hold machine guns to the
heads of drowning terrorized people, no reason to leave
folks waving desperately from rooftops, no reason to
raise the rent on houses that don't exist, no reason
to do any of this if we had all been raised believing the
end goal was kindness. We are taught instead it is about
money, power, privilege, security. How harsh this hunt
for security makes us, how cruel. It teaches us to take
care of ourselves, our own. Not to go too far out, not
to go outside a certain circle. Katrina washed away all
these illusions, all this veneer.

New Orleans is still standing because of Katrina
warriors who sacrificed the little they did have to give
more.

Charmaine Marchand, the state representative of the
Lower Ninth and Ninth Wards, is a fierce and inspired
woman. She leads the community meeting every Sat-
urday. She told me, "They bring everyone down to the
Ninth Ward to show the terrible damage in order to get
money. They use us to get money and then they don't
give it to us." Eight months after Katrina, there was still
no electricity or water. The government was refusing to
give people the money they needed to rebuild their
houses. "They are not going to nickel-and-dime us,"
she told her community. "The levee breached. This

wasn't our fault. They need to fix our houses. If poor folks don't qualify, who does? You can't be scared to speak up." In the meeting, she organized buses to take people to Baton Rouge to meet with the governor. She told them, "You want to come back. You need to come back. You want your money. Then go get your money. We built the bridges. We built the buildings and roads in New Orleans. We gave our blood and sweat and tears. This is our city. They cannot call you a refugee when you gave your heart and soul to America." Her spirit was contagious and the people in the room were speaking out.

Sandrah was watering her plants and getting her grandson to private school for $230 a month, even though it was most of her money. She proudly showed me the pots of growing green life in every window. "I take care of my plants. I love them and my grandson. I can watch them grow. I know I've done something good." Ecoee was organizing the nurses in Lord & Taylor in the sexual-assault unit. Because of poverty, trauma, lack of jobs, and alcoholism, violence against women was rapidly on the rise. She was helping relieve stress in every person she touched and building programs in spite of the fact that the hospital was in a former department store.

Patricia told me she was hurting. She said she

dreamed of winning the lottery so she could take care of all the suffering people. She said her church was her life and her church was very, very damaged. She said she used to cook oxtails there in the kitchen every Thursday for the homeless. She was lost without her cooking.

Several days later, Patricia and her pastor, Reverend Eugene James, brought me to see their church. It was a simple jewel box in the middle of a crumbling community. The pastor was visibly crushed when we walked through the door, even though he had been cleaning it out for weeks. It was the showing of it that destroyed his heart and pride. "There was red carpet here," he said, pointing to the decimated floors. "And there was red velvet covering the pew seats."

The photocopied sign on the naked church wall read JESUS, GATHERING UP THE FRAGMENTS THAT RE-MAIN SO THAT NOTHING WILL BE LOST. I think about how there are no places—no churches, schools, or community centers—left in New Orleans for gathering. I think about how impossible it is for humans to get their bearings or power or meaning without gathering. I think maybe the closest we get to the feeling of security is in the gathering, the coming together, becoming a group, a community, a whole.

We cannot prevent disasters, but we can be there with and for one another when they occur. We can extend our hand, we can remember those who have lost their homes, their jobs, their minds, and their way. We can help those who can't help themselves, we can spend the money fixing the levee rather than building military installations for illegal wars, we can offer blankets when soaking, traumatized people cross our bridge rather than turning them back. We can send buses to poor folks' neighborhoods before the storm hits, we can make a commitment to end poverty itself, we can bring water and food and hammers and nails to rebuild the broken walls.

For the folks in New Orleans that would be a way out of hell.

CONCLUSION:
PEACE IS A STATE OF BEING; SECURITY IS BEING OF THE STATE

The Law of Security goes something like this. It is almost a guarantee that in the pursuit of security you will become more insecure. Inherent in the quest for security is its undoing. Some recent examples: bomb Iraq to get rid of theoretical terrorists and manufacture thousands of potential terrorists in the process. Send American soldiers into battle in Iraq to make the country secure, but refuse to spend any money on armor to make the soldiers secure, so that 80 percent of those who receive upper-body wounds die of injuries that could have been prevented. Declare war on Iraq to get rid of chemical weapons and end up using illegal chemical weapons (incendiary devices) that destroy the children you are saving. Secure democracy by using techniques of torture that not only thoroughly undermine democracy but spread distrust, contempt, rage, and violence, which will forever make democracy impossible. In securing freedom, rob citizens everywhere of their basic civil rights, imprison them without trial or recourse, hold them for as long as you like without charging them. Put them in invisible prisons in countries that you once claimed were responsible for gulags. Wiretap private citizens without a warrant and by doing so expand presidential powers so they become Imperial Powers and strip the so-called democracy you were defending. Promise to liberate women through your invasion and occupation and in the process reverse their constitutional rights, rob them of protection, raise the levels of violence permitted toward them. Spend all of your money on security and end up with the hugest deficit ever, no health care for the majority of citizens, no protection against disasters, no vaccines for a potential flu plague. Make the world "secure" by spending all of your money on destroying things rather than creating—bomb rather than build, annihilate rather than feed. Focus your attention on imagined enemies who must be controlled or destroyed and in the process make them your real enemies. Rescue people from insane dictators by terrorizing them.

Allow corporations to ransack countries you are, in theory, saving, making the majority of the people poor and sick and without resources, then call them security threats, illegal combatants, terrorists, insurgents, when they rise up to fight you.

In "securing" people, make them really really afraid. Create all kinds of colors and alerts that terrorize the population. Terror and numbness will eventually be mistaken for security. In "securing" people, take away their opinions and voices and instincts. Make them feel afraid to speak out. Control will eventually be mistaken for security. In "securing" people, distract them through addictive consumption and mindless entertainment programming. Amnesia will eventually be mistaken for security.

Freedom can come only from contemplating death, not from pretending it doesn't exist. Not from running from loss but from entering grief, surrendering to sorrow.

Freedom comes not from holding your life more precious or sacred than others'. Not from consuming more than your share.

Freedom is not knowing something when you don't know it.

Freedom means I may not be identified with any one group, but I can visit and find myself in every group. Freedom does not mean I don't have values or beliefs. But it does mean I am not hardened around them. I do not use them as weapons.

Freedom cannot be bought or arranged or made with bombs or guards. It is deeper. It is a process. It is the acute awareness that we are all utterly interdependent. That economic injustice and inequity creates an environment of global despair and rage that, until balanced, will inevitably lead to hatred and violence.

Freedom is not only being able to tolerate mystery, complexity, ambiguity, but hungering for them and only trusting a situation when they are present.

Not owned, not occupied, not bought.

Finding the place in me that connects with every person I meet rather than being different, better, or on top.

Believing there is a power determining everything at the same moment that I know there is absolutely no one in charge.

Wanting to win the award when I know awards mean nothing.

Freedom is not knowing where you are but being deeply there.

Not waiting for someone to save or rescue you or make up for your terrible past. Doing that for yourself.

Not putting your flag in the ground.

Not owning people or ideas. Being willing to get lost in the desert.

Freedom is about becoming vulnerable to one another, rather than becoming secure, in control, and alone.

The increasing insecurity of the world can make us

insane or can simply clarify reality, which is that we are going to die and it could happen anytime, anywhere.

The world is indeed a near-death experience, forcing us, if we let it, to let go of certain illusions that separate us from one another. Having this in our consciousness could be the elixir that makes us more feeling, more present, more appreciative, more loving, more generous.

It is clear that the tactics of this current regime— retaliation, humiliation, and revenge—have actually increased terrorist attacks in the world and undermined security. There were more terrorist attacks in 2004 than in any year since 1985.

"People across the world overwhelmingly believe the war in Iraq has increased the likelihood of terrorist attacks worldwide," revealed a poll for the BBC in March 2006. "Some sixty percent of people in thirty-five countries surveyed believe this is the case, against just twelve percent who think terrorist attacks have become less likely."

But, more important, most of the dying in this world, most of the suffering, is not a result of terrorism. The focus on terrorism has been one of the great manipulations and diversions. Most of the people of the world, particularly outside the U.S., live in perilous conditions. The greed-centered economic policies of multinational corporations in partnership with the U.S. government masquerading as our great protectors cause worldwide starvation, the destruction of the environment, horrendous poverty, illness, illiteracy, the spreading of AIDS, and resulting violence.

If we are truly interested in security, let's begin with securing all people the basic human right to food, shelter, drinkable water, health care, a place to live, safety, and a livable earth.

Let's take that $250 billion (which could ultimately become $1.3 trillion) that it cost to bomb the heart out of Iraq, to murder the children there, to kill and maim thousands of people, to scatter ready-to-explode cluster bomblets on the Iraqi earth, to fill the bank accounts of the CEOs at Halliburton and Bechtel. Let's take that money and make compassion the end goal, human connection the end goal, honoring all people the end goal.

Then, I promise, we may not know security, but we will certainly know peace.

ACKNOWLEDGMENTS

Thanks to Kim Rosen, for thirty-three years of teaching me to fall, and for her relentless pursuit of correct comma placement; to Paula Allen, for inspiring me to go out there in the first place; to Nancy Miller, for encouraging me and helping me greatly to make this something whole; to Charlotte Sheedy, for her fierceness, vision, and loyalty.

To David Stone, for defying gravity.

To Jane Fonda, who blazed the trail for me; to Pat Mitchell, for her generosity in everything; and to Diana de Vegh, who believed from the beginning.

To my V sisters, who have taught me what can happen when people live in their hearts and give completely, driven by the hunger to end violence: Jerri Lynn Fields, Susan Swan, Hibaaq Osman, Allison Prouty, Cecile Lipworth, Shael Norris, and Amy Squires.

To Kate Fisher, who generously and thoroughly researched the facts, for her willingness to leap in and go there.

To Tony Montenieri, for his deep care on the journey across the country that made this book.

To James Lecesne, Clive Flowers, Rada Boric, Mark Matousek, Brenda Currin, Elizabeth Lesser, Mollie Doyle, Judy Corcoran, Nicoletta Billi, Marie Cecile Renaud, Carole Black, John Ruskin, and Anthony Arnove.

To Harriet Leve, who believed good could be great; and to Nancy Rose, George Lane, and Frank Selvaggi, for being in my corner.

To Manhattanville College, where this book was born.

To all the Vagina Warriors I met on this journey, who taught me compassion, fierceness, and love. To the women in my group at Bedford Hills Correctional Facility, that you may soon be free. To Sister Elaine Roulet, who wakes each day to end suffering.

To my granddaughters, Coco and Charlotte McDermott; my nieces, Hannah and Katherine Ensler; my goddaughters, Molly Kawachi, Lulu Mazur, and Azariah Blunt; my adopted daughters, Adisa Krupalija and Zoya; and my loved one, Harriet Clark—may you all be willing to jump, dive, or fall.

To my mother, Chris.

To my sister, Laura.

To my brother, Curtis.

To my daughter-in-law, Shiva, for her tenderness.

To my son, Dylan, who melted me.

To my father, Arthur, who broke me . . . open.

EVE ENSLER is an internationally acclaimed playwright whose works for the stage include *Floating Rhoda and the Glue Man, Lemonade, Necessary Targets, The Vagina Monologues,* and *The Good Body.* Ensler is the founder and artistic director of V-Day (www.vday.org), the global movement to end violence against women and girls that was inspired by *The Vagina Monologues.* In ten years V-Day has raised more than $50 million for grassroots groups around the world. Eve Ensler lives in New York City.